MICROFORM SETS IN

U.S. AND CANADIAN LIBRARIES

Report of a Survey on the Bibliographic Control
of Microform Sets Conducted by the Association of
Research Libraries Microform Project

Compiled by
Jeffrey Heynen, Coordinator
ARL Microform Project
503 11th Street, SE
Washington, DC 20003
(202) 544-0291

Association of Research Libraries
Washington, D.C.
1984

ISBN 0-918006-08-2

TABLE OF CONTENTS

Appendices

Microform Sets in U.S. and Canadian Libraries

Introduction

The Association of Research Libraries Microform Project has recently established a clearinghouse on the bibliographic control of microforms. Libraries that are now cataloging microform collections of books and serials and libraries that are planning new microform cataloging projects should contact the Project office for details regarding cataloging records that may already be available for titles in the microform sets which concern them.

Libraries may use clearinghouse data to locate records on the bibliographic utilities or they may use the data to acquire tapes of machine-readable cataloging from other libraries for loading into in-house systems. Information is also available on records that have been coded for set processing and that can thus be automatically updated to include local library identification and local call numbers for acquisition in collated sets of cards or pre-processed tapes. Other information in the clearinghouse data base includes what sets are held and whether local finding tools have been prepared for them as well as details regarding cataloging that has been given titles contained in the sets. In all, the data base contains information given by 535 responding libraries in up to 68 separate categories.

In addition to helping libraries to catalog titles in microform sets and to acquire automatically-profiled cataloging records for sets, this information may be used to create cooperative cataloging projects, prevent duplicated effort, compile state-wide or regional union lists of microform holdings, and draft microform cataloging grant applications.

The clearinghouse is a major program of the Microform Project. This report describes the background of the project and summarizes results of the survey from which the clearinghouse data base has been constructed.

Background

Commercial and nonprofit organizations have been re-publishing collections of books and serials in microfilm, microfiche, and other microformats for nearly half a century. Both publication and acquisition of these microform sets increased dramatically in the 1960s and early 1970s, and more recently, while acquisition rates of books and serials in hardcopy format leveled off or declined, acquisition rates of microform publications remained at high levels. As a result, microform unit holdings in many libraries currently equal or exceed volume counts of hardcopy books and serials. Although there are no statistics giving truly comparable holdings data -- such as numbers of titles or pages of both hardcopy and microform publications -- it is plain nonetheless that microform sets now constitute a very significant portion of overall library resources.

Microform Sets in U.S. and Canadian Libraries

Despite this prominence, microform sets are notoriously under-used. Recent improvements in the design and operation of microform reading rooms have been useful, but not in themselves sufficient to overcome the problem. Attempts to increase usage by means of annotated bibliographies, checklists, and guides have only partly improved matters, and indexes and abstracting services (which have been useful in providing access to individual serials and government publications in microform) have proven both unaffordable and impractical when applied to microform sets.

Full, title-by-title cataloging of the works contained in these sets has the potential for increasing usage dramatically. Nonetheless, the task of providing catalog records for each title in all the sets of every library collection has, until recently, seemed impossibly difficult. The Library of Congress has not (until very recently) been a source for microform cataloging, and the catalog card sets provided by most microform publishers and some enterprising libraries have been difficult to adapt for local use.

The evolution of on-line shared cataloging within large bibliographic utilities created an opportunity for overcoming this impasse. Such cataloging provides the means for dividing the work load and sharing the work product so that microforms may be given full cataloging in accordance with widely-accepted standards in an extremely efficient and cost-effective manner.

Recognizing this fact, in 1976-78 R. Grey Cole chaired a subcommittee of the Resources Section Micropublishing Committee (American Library Association, Resources and Technical Services Division) which developed a program for using cataloging networks to achieve bibliographic control of microforms. Drawing on the advice of representatives from libraries, microform publishers, grant-making organizations, and the Library of Congress, the subcommittee produced a strategy that led, in 1979, to the creation of an ARL planning study which led in turn to the establishment of the ARL Microform Project.

The project got underway in August 1981 with grants from the Council on Library Resources and the Andrew W. Mellon Foundation. Recently the Mellon Foundation made ARL a further grant to operate the microform cataloging clearinghouse on a part-time basis through September 1984.

Objectives of the ARL Microform Project

The project aims to assist libraries and microform publishers in their creation of machine-readable cataloging records for the many thousands of titles in microform sets that have heretofore either not been cataloged or inadequately cataloged. As major tools in accomplishing this task, the project has been pursuing the establishment of set-processing (or profile-matching) mechanisms whereby records are coded to permit their being accessed en masse with automatic addition of local data. Once coded for set processing, machine-readable records for a given set can be manipulated as a separate file. Libraries can request the bibliographic utility that holds the records to process them as a set, adding local identifying information and call numbers in a single machine operation and supplying cards and/or tapes as needed. Unit costs for this service should be far less than the cost for use of machine-readable cataloging on a title-by-title basis.

In addition to the creation of set processing mechanisms, the goals of the project include the following: (a) providing information to libraries on machine-readable records that are available for them to use in copy cataloging, (b) assisting libraries to establish cooperative projects to catalog sets for which individual library cataloging is impractical, (c) pursuit of arrangements among the bibliographic utilities for sharing microform cataloging records, (d) encouraging the production of high-quality machine-readable records by microform publishers, (e) fostering improved bibliographic tools for preservation microfilming, and (f) working to achieve consensus on cataloging standards for microform cataloging.

Progress Toward Achieving the Objectives

The basic goals of the project have been achieved or are well on the way to accomplishment. A surprising number of major microform cataloging projects are underway in U.S. and Canadian libraries. For example, 41 of the 85 sets that were given highest-priority for cataloging in the Microform Project survey are already fully cataloged in machine-readable form or are in the process of becoming fully cataloged on either the Online Computer Library Center (OCLC) network or the Research Libraries Information Network (RLIN). This cataloging does not entirely result from the work of the project, of course, but much of it has come about as a result of the Coordinator's work and of the publicity surrounding the investigations that preceded the project.

OCLC has established a set-processing system and should soon announce its access and pricing policies. Information regarding the system, which is called "Major Microforms," is available from OCLC's Eileen Henthorne. Sets cataloged under Higher Education Act Title II-C grants by the University of Utah and Indiana University, as well as a set being cooperatively cataloged, have been or are being coded for set processing. Further coding for set-processing is planned both for new cataloging and for cataloging that has already been entered into OCLC.

Under the auspices of the Microform Cataloging Task Force of OCLC's Research Libraries Advisory Committee (RLAC), a joint cooperative project is underway for cataloging the Research Publications microform set entitled American Fiction. This is the set for which cataloging records are being coded for set processing as noted above. Further joint cataloging projects are being planned by the Task Force and its chair, W. David Laird, Director of the University of Arizona Library.

The Coordinator has worked closely with the RLAC cooperative group, with the libraries that have been cataloging microform sets under HEA Title II-C grants, with the Library of Congress, and with other libraries that are establishing new microform cataloging programs.

Microform Sets in U.S. and Canadian Libraries

OCLC and the Research Libraries Group (RLG) have agreed to exchange computer tapes for microform cataloging that has been done using Title II-C grants. (Stanford University, an RLG member, has also received II-C microform cataloging grants.)

Although the publication of new microform sets seems to have leveled off or declined, and the microform publishing industry appears to be in a period of consolidation, one major publisher, University Microfilms International (UMI), continues to produce a high volume of machine-readable records using OCLC and is expected to negotiate set-processing arrangements with OCLC. Another major publisher, Research Publications (RP), is expected to begin OCLC cataloging in the near future. Both UMI and RP are providing support to libraries that are cataloging sets they have already published. Other publishers have agreed to take similar roles with respect to the sets they have published.

The Coordinator has been working closely with the Library of Congress in its planning for the integration of the National Register of Microform Masters and Newspapers in Microfilm into the new NUC publishing program. This and other preservation-related work has been expanded within the NEH-funded preservation microfilming component of the Microform Project (begun in the fall of 1982 and continuing on a half-time basis until the fall of 1984).

Basic problems concerning cataloging standards were effectively solved when the Library of Congress issued its interpretation of AACR 2 with respect to microforms. The Coordinator has worked with LC and with ALA's Interdivisional Committee on Representation in Machine-Readable Form of Bibliographic Information (MARBI) in revising and re-defining the MARC 007 Physical Description Fixed Field for microforms and he continues to work with standards-making bodies, such as the PH5 and Z39 committees of the American National Standards Institute (ANSI), concerning standards on microform matters.

Information Clearinghouse

In 1982, the ARL Microform Project conducted a survey to obtain detailed information regarding the bibliographic control of microform sets that are held by U.S. and Canadian libraries. Survey results have been used to establish a computerized clearinghouse having three components: (1) information on overall library policies relating to the cataloging of titles in microform sets, (2) information on individual library holdings of specific sets and on the bibliographic control given to them, and (3) information on individual library priorities for cataloging specific sets and interest in cooperative projects to catalog them.

Libraries and microform publishers that are currently cataloging titles in microform sets or that are planning to start new cataloging programs may call or write the project office for reports on sets that concern them. These reports show whether or not cataloging has already been given to a specific set, and, if so, give such details as the proportion of the set that has been cataloged, the main source and level of cataloging, and the cataloging code observed. Where titles have been provided with machine-readable cataloging, they show the proportion cataloged, whether cataloging continues, whether tapes are held locally, and into which data bases records have been entered. In addition, reports provide information on machine-readable cataloging that has been given sets; they show the proportion of each set that has been given machine-readable cataloging, whether creation of machine-readable records continues, and whether tapes are held locally. They also show the data bases into which records have been entered and whether the records have been tagged for set processing.

Libraries can use this information to catalog titles in microform sets that they hold or are in the process of acquiring. Records that have been coded for set processing will soon be available from OCLC in card or tape form. Records that have not been coded for set processing may be used as sources for cataloging title-by-title on the utilities on which they are found. Libraries that have on-line catalogs and/or in-house data processing capability may use the clearinghouse to locate and acquire cataloging tapes that are held by other libraries.

Other clearinghouse functions include the following: (1) providing data useful in putting together groups for cooperative cataloging projects, such as the RLAC cooperative project to catalog the American Fiction microfilm set; (2) preventing duplication of effort; (3) supporting applications for cataloging grants, for example under the HEA Title II-C program; (4) setting priorities for cataloging; (5) providing a link between publishers and libraries in matters concerning microform cataloging; and (6) compiling union lists of microform holdings on state-wide, regional, or other bases.

In the six months since the Clearinghouse began operations, the Coordinator has responded to over 100 requests for information. These range from questions that can be answered within a single telephone conversation to queries that require the production of lengthy reports detailing data base subsets for whole categories of respondents (e.g. all RLIN users). Since the production of the latter may require more than a few days of effort, and since the the Clearinghouse is funded to operate only nine hours per week, Clearinghouse operations have, so far, significantly exceeded expectations.

Description of the Survey

The survey took its form from two earlier surveys: one conducted by ARL's Office of Management Studies (OMS) in 1979 and the other by the ARL planning consultants, Information Systems Consultants Inc. (ISCI), in 1980. It was drafted, reviewed, tested, and revised during the spring of 1982. Its questionnaire consists of three parts, the first on library microform cataloging policies, the second on holdings and bibliographic control of specific microform sets, and the third on cataloging priorities for specific sets and interest in projects for cataloging them. A copy of the survey questionnaire may be found at the end of this report before the appendices.

Microform Sets in U.S. and Canadian Libraries

The survey was originally to be distributed only to groups of large research libraries for which mailing lists were available, i.e. members of ARL, the Canadian Association of Research Libraries (CARL), the Independent Research Libraries Association (IRLA), RLG, and the 103 libraries, next-largest after those in ARL, which are covered in the Association of College and Research Libraries (ACRL) publication: ACRL University Library Statistics (ACRL, Chicago, IL, 1980). However, the cooperation of the major bibliographic utilities -- OCLC, RLG (RLIN), WLN, and UTLAS -- permitted it to be sent to all of their participants. Because the distribution of the survey was thus extremely broad, many of its recipients were libraries that hold no microform sets. Almost 200 respondents indicated that the survey did not apply to them for this reason. A few others stated that they did not have the resources to complete the survey forms.

The following table gives totals of survey recipients by affiliation. As a courtesy, ARL sent surveys to directors of ARL and CARL member libraries even though the utilities in which they participate would also send surveys to designated staff members. This overlapping distribution was explained in cover memos and caused no known confusion among recipients.

Table 1, Distribution Summary

Organization	Number of Recipients
Association of Research Libraries	113
CARL members, other than ARL members	18
RLG Members and RLIN users, other than ARL members	85*
OCLC Participants	3000**
UTLAS Participants	370
WLN Participants	90
	3676

Respondent Profiles

The following tables show the number of responses received up to September 15, 1983 from various categories of libraries that completed and returned the survey forms. Not all libraries returned each of the three parts of the

----

* At the time the survey was distributed, RLIN users apart from RLG members included 13 law and art libraries and 69 participants in the Cooperative Library Agency for Systems and Services (CLASS) network. One RLG member is not also an ARL member.

** This is an estimate. OCLC, which generously provided printing and mailing services for this group of recipients, could not provide an exact distribution count.

survey questionnaire. The project has received 509 returns of Part II
(containing details on holdings and bibliographic control of specific sets)
and 267 returns of Part III (containing data on priorities for cataloging and
on interest in projects for cooperatively cataloging specific sets). A total
of 535 returns include Part I (on cataloging policies) and at least one other
Part. This last total is taken as the number of substantive responses to the
survey as shown below. Appendix A contains a full list of these 535
respondents by institution. Appendix B lists them by NUC Symbol.

Because the survey data base is not a fixed entity, the numbers given
below are not final figures. The data base is revised and updated as new
information is obtained. Libraries that wish to submit new information should
contact the project office to obtain forms. The project's address and
telephone number are given on the title page of this report.

Table 2 categorizes respondents by type of libraries. Not surprisingly,
72% of responding libraries are in academic institutions that offer Bachelors'
or higher degrees. These libraries have always comprised the largest customer
base for published microform sets and they expanded their holdings more
rapidly than others during the high-acquisition period of the 1960s and 1970s.

Table 2, Profile of Respondents by Type of Library

University Libraries	270
Four-Year College Libraries	113
Government Libraries	35
Law Libraries	34
Public Libraries	23
Theological Libraries	13
Medical Libraries	9
Art Libraries	7
Special Libraries	5
Two-Year College Libraries	4
Music Libraries	1
School Libraries and Others	21

	535

Table 3a confirms another expected result of the survey: that large
research libraries -- most of which are, of course, academic libraries -- are
also likely to have extensive holdings of microform sets and therefore are
likely to make the considerable effort required to complete the survey
response forms.

Although Table 3a seems to suggest that a total of 288 large research
libraries were sent survey questionnaires, elimination of multiple
affiliations reduces the actual total to 237. The ARL and ACRL lists are
mutually exclusive, but at the time the survey was distributed, 12 CARL
members were also ARL members and nine others were on the ACRL list. In
addition, four IRLA members and 26 RLG members are also ARL members. One RLG
member is also an IRLA member. The number of responses received from these

237 libraries was 180 (a rate of return of 76%). Twenty-five of the 57 non-respondents sent replies stating either that they held no sets (most of the IRLA non-respondents are in this category) or that they did not have the resources to respond (most of the CARL non-respondents). The reply rate for large research libraries is thus 205 of 237, or 86%. Appendix C is a list of the 32 large research libraries that have, so far, returned no response forms and sent no other reply.

Large research libraries that hold sets and that have not yet replied or that have replied but have not yet completed survey response forms may still participate in the survey. Questionnaires are available from the project office.

Table 3a, Profile of Respondents by Membership Affiliation

	Survey Returns	Member-ship	No Re-sponse	No Reply
ARL members	103	113	3	7
ACRL (103 lgst. non-ARL memb.)	69	103	10	24
CARL members	23	30	5	2
IRLA members	7	15	5	3
RLG members	26	27	1	0

Key: **Survey Returns**: libraries that returned Part I and at least one other Part. **Membership**: level at time of survey distribution. **No Response**: Libraries that sent replies indicating that they could not respond to the survey either because they hold no sets or because they do not have staff time for completing the survey forms. **No Reply**: Libraries that made no reply.

Table 3b, Profile of Respondents by Participation in Bibliographic Utility

RLG members	27
Other RLIN participants	8
OCLC participants	420
WLN participants	15
UTLAS participants	37

Based on the level of membership at the time the survey was conducted, the current response rate for ARL members is 90%. The response rate for the ACRL group is 67%; for CARL members it is 77%, for IRLA it is 47%, and for RLG, 96%. OCLC participants represent 78% of respondents; UTLAS participants, 7%; RLG members and other RLIN participants, 6%; and WLN participants, 3%. Twenty-nine respondents (5%) either do not belong to a bibliographic utility or did not give information permitting their participation to be entered into the data base.

Microform Sets in U.S. and Canadian Libraries

Responses to Part I: Microform Cataloging Policies

Summary. Part I of the survey questionnaire is framed in a multiple-choice format. Respondents are asked to put check marks showing the applicable response to each of the form's eight questions. This part of the questionnaire has elements in common with the 1979 OMS survey. Interestingly, the OMS survey, whose distribution was limited to ARL member libraries, shows that 92% of responding libraries sometimes or always create records for titles in microform sets while the Microform Project survey shows 71% of its respondents sometimes or always do so. The Microform Project's inclusion of many smaller libraries with limited cataloging departments may account for the difference in these two figures. Similarly, the OMS survey shows that 64% of respondents enter records into a machine-readable data base, while the Microform Project survey shows that 50% do so.

Questions and Response Totals. Information given by libraries in completing Part I of the Microform Project survey can be usefully summarized by tallying the responses given to each response option. These totals are given below together with the questions to which they pertain.

1. Does the library catalog some or all of the titles that are contained within large microform sets and/or provide full analytics for sets?
   Always: 45   **Sometimes: 335**   **Never: 136**

2. Do you catalog titles in sets already held and/or catalog new acquisitions?
   Sets already held: 204   **New acquisitions: 340**

3. Has the library in the past entered this cataloging into one or more machine-readable data bases?
   Always: 75   **Sometimes: 169**   **Never: 222**

4. Does the library continue to enter this cataloging into a machine-readable data base?
   Yes: 269

5. Into which data base(s) have you entered or do you enter microform cataloging records?
   Formerly: OCLC, 151; RLIN, 5; WLN, 3; UTLAS, 16; In-House, 26; Other, 3
   Currently: OCLC, 203; RLIN, 22; WLN, 5; UTLAS, 20; In-House, 33; Other, 10

6. If the library catalogs titles within microform sets as they are acquired, do you keep records showing what sets receive cataloging and how many titles have been cataloged? **Yes: 179   No/No Response: 356**

7. Does the library use catalog cards supplied by publishers when they are available?
   Always: 66   **Sometimes: 235**   **Never: 184**

8. If the library does use catalog cards supplied by publishers, are these records substantially revised before being used?
   Always: 37   **Sometimes: 170**   **Never: 110**

Microform Sets in U.S. and Canadian Libraries

The responses to Part I of the Microform Project survey show some interesting results. The number of libraries that sometimes or always catalog titles in microform sets is high (380 respondents). Although a large number of libraries catalog sets already held and sets newly acquired, considerably more libraries catalog new acquisitions than catalog existing holdings.

119 libraries reported that they sometimes or always catalog titles in microform sets but have not in the past entered and are not currently entering records into a machine-readable data base. Of this group, 19 libraries that always catalog sets have never in the past entered records, though nine of them currently enter them. 129 libraries that sometimes catalog sets never entered records in the past, though 20 of these currently enter them. 220 libraries never in the past created machine-readable records for titles in microform sets. One always created them in the past but does not currently do so, and eight report that they sometimes in the past entered records for sets into a data base but do not now do so.

A higher proportion of libraries is shown to continue to enter records into a machine-readable data base than is shown to have produced machine-readable cataloging in the past (64% versus 46%), suggesting that the production of machine-readable cataloging for titles in microform sets is a fast-growing practice. OCLC, not surprisingly, is the dominant data base into which records have been or are being entered. As the table on the following page shows, 37% of all respondents currently enter records for titles in microform sets into OCLC. However, a higher proportion of RLIN and UTLAS participants currently enter records into their data bases than do OCLC participants into OCLC.

A total of 32 libraries reported current entry of records into more than one data base. A total of 18 reported entry into an in-house system as well as one of the bibliographic utilities. Eight reported entry into a system designated "other" as well as into a utility (most of these "other" data bases may be systems such as GEAC). Five reported entry into both OCLC and RLIN.

Table 4. Proportion of libraries that enter
records into machine-readable data bases.

Category of Respondent	Data Base	Proportion of Libraries Entering Records Into a Machine-Readable Data Base	
		Currently	Formerly
All respondents (n=535)	Any of them	50%	46%
	OCLC	37%	28%
	RLIN	4%	1%
	UTLAS	4%	3%
	WLN	1%	1%
	In-House	3%	3%
Respondents that currently create machine-readable records (n=269)	OCLC	74%	56%
	RLIN	7%	1%
	UTLAS	7%	6%
	WLN	2%	1%
	In-House	6%	7%
OCLC participants (n=420)	OCLC	48%	36%
RLG members and RLIN participants (n=34)	RLIN	56%	12%
UTLAS participants (n=37)	UTLAS	54%	43%
WLN participants (n=15)	WLN	33%	20%

As expected, libraries are cautious in their response to cataloging
provided by publishers. Thirty-four percent of respondents never use it and
44% use it with discretion. A high proportion of those that use publishers'
cataloging do so only after substantial revision (65%).

Responses to Part II: Holdings and Bibliographic Control of Specific Sets

Summary. Part II of the questionnaire is a form having a grid pattern on
which respondents are requested (1) to insert numeric identifiers for each
microform set which they hold and (2) to respond to the following instructions
insofar as they apply and the data are available.

   1. Hold entire set: Put a check mark if library has all
parts of set that have been published, publishing has ceased,
and holdings are complete.
   2. Hold approximately ___% of set: For sets that are
incompletely held and not still being received: give

approximate proportion of set held.

3. Still receive portions: Put a check mark if set is still being acquired on standing order or subscription (but not if library intends to acquire additional, but entirely separate parts for which different code numbers are provided).

4. Have prepared local finding tools for set: Put a check mark if library has prepared finding tools other than catalog records for the titles which the set contains.

5. Have cataloged titles in set: Put a check mark if the library has cataloged, or analyzed, all of the titles that the set contains.

6. Cataloging continues: Put a check mark if cataloging of this set is still in process.

7. Approximate % of titles cataloged: Give the approximate percentage of titles owned that have been cataloged.

8. Main source of cataloging copy: Indicate whether the main source of cataloging copy was the microform publisher ("P"), the National Union Catalog or LC catalogs ("N"), a shared-cataloging bibliographic data base ("B"), or another source ("X").

9. Cataloging code: Indicate whether the main code followed was pre-AACR2 ("P"), AACR2 ("2"), or neither of them ("X").

10. Level of cataloging: Show, broadly, whether records are full ("F"), minimal level ("M"), or brief ("B"). Full means in accordance with the library's policies for full level cataloging. Minimal level means in accordance with the national minimal level standard. Brief means neither of these.

11. Percentage entered into data base: Give the approximate percentage of titles owned for which records have been entered into an in-house machine-readable data base or a shared-cataloging data base such as OCLC, RLIN, WLN, or UTLAS.

12. Entering continues: Put a check mark if the library continues to enter records for the set into a data base.

13. Hold tapes locally: Put a check mark if library has local holdings of machine-readable records for the set.

14. Specify data bases: Indicate the data base(s) into which records for the set have been entered: "O" for OCLC, "R" for RLIN, "W" for WLN, "U" for UTLAS, "I" for in-house, and "X" for other.

Responses on Non-Machine-Readable Cataloging. The following tables summarize data provided by libraries in response to the 14 categories on Part II's response form. In the first table, the total given for each response is the number of instances that the response was given by a library. In addition to this total, the second table provides totals by set and by library. Where libraries could not supply data, they either left the response block blank or put a question mark, and the totals are thus indicative but not absolute numbers.

Microform Sets in U.S. and Canadian Libraries

The total number of holdings reported by respondents is 11,289. The largest number of sets held by a single library is 164. Nine libraries reported holdings greater than 100 sets, and the average number of sets held is 22.

A total of 809 different sets were identified, 448 of them from a listing supplied with the questionnaire and 361 added to the listing by respondents. No holdings were reported for 35 of the 483 sets in the listing that accompanies the questionnaire. Appendix D is a list of sets for which holdings were reported. Appendix E contains sets for which no holdings were reported.

Table 5 shows that 13% of holdings have been given some form of local finding tool and 24% have been completely cataloged in some form. The source used for most cataloging is shown to be publisher-supplied copy (37% of holdings for which data on cataloging source was supplied).

A high proportion of cataloged holdings have been given full cataloging (2,188 or 72% of the 3,033 for which data on level of cataloging has been given). In contrast, 18% of this group received brief cataloging and 10% received minimal-level cataloging.

Table 5, Summary of Responses to Part II on Non-Machine-Readable Cataloging

Category	No. of Responses (i.e. Holdings)
Hold Entire Set –	6,482
Hold Part of Set – sets not still being received –	2,605
Still Receive Portions –	2,463
Have Prepared Local Finding Tools for Set –	1,464
Have Cataloged –	2,708
Cataloging Continues –	726
Main Cataloging Source is/was publisher –	1,092
LC/NUC is/was Main Source –	894
Data base Apart From Publisher's or LC Copy –	297
Any Other Source –	684
Main Cataloging Code is Pre-AACR2 –	2,371
Main Code is AACR2 –	255
Other Code –	305
Cataloging Level is Full –	2,188
Level is Minimal –	299
Level is Brief –	546

Responses on Machine-Readable Cataloging. The most valuable responses to Part II of the survey concern machine-readable cataloging that has been provided for titles within sets. The table on the following page summarizes responses on this topic. Note that at least some machine-readable cataloging has been created for a fairly high proportion of sets (40%) and that the majority of this cataloging is available on OCLC (71%).

In 191 instances, libraries have entered records for a set into two data bases. In some cases specific titles have been cataloged on both data bases; more commonly, some titles have been cataloged on the first and some on the second. The most frequent combination of data bases is OCLC and in-house (15 instances), followed by RLIN and in-house (10 instances).

Fifty-eight percent of the 321 sets that have been given any machine-readable cataloging are reported to have been completely cataloged in machine-readable form. The cataloging of 55% is reported to be in process. Although these proportions are surprisingly high, they do not reflect the true volume of completed and in-process machine-readable cataloging since a number of libraries did not know whether or not cataloging was complete at time of reporting and thus left these items blank or inserted question marks in them.

The sum of the two percentages is greater than 100 mainly as a result of the entering of records for a given set into two or more different data bases, but also because libraries reported the copy cataloging of sets as well as original cataloging of them, because libraries sometimes prefer newly created records of their own making to those already available on a shared cataloging data base, and presumably also because there is some degree of unintentional duplication of cataloging effort.

Table 6 shows that 46% of the 509 libraries returning Part II of the survey have created at least some machine-readable records and that 73% of libraries that created any machine-readable records have done so on OCLC. Fifty-two percent of libraries that have created any machine-readable records have completely cataloged at least one set, and 31% of the libraries in this group continue to enter records into a data base.

Data given in response to Part II is not entirely consistent with responses to Part I. For example, Part II shows that 269 libraries currently enter records into a data base, while only 235 libraries reporting entry of records for specific sets in Part II. Part I shows current entry of records into OCLC by 200 libraries, while only 172 libraries report entering records for specific sets into OCLC.

These discrepancies are partly explained by the fact that 26 libraries returned Part I of the questionnaire, but not Part II. They are also explained by the imperfect administrative records with which respondents had to work in many cases. Apparently, some respondents to Part I believed their libraries to be creating machine-readable records for titles in microform sets, but the respondent to Part II (not necessarily the same person) could not identify the set being given this cataloging.

Table 6, Summary of Machine-Readable Cataloging
of Microform Sets from Part II of the Survey

	Holdings	Sets	Libraries
Machine-readable records have been created (any at all)	942	321	235
Machine-readable records have been entered into:			
OCLC	569	227	172
an in-house system	163	81	30
UTLAS	72	54	18
RLIN	71	54	16
WLN	10	10	3
SOLINET	6	6	1
other	26	24	7
unknown	61	56	34
Entering of machine-readable records for set is complete	341	185	123
Entering of machine-readable records for set continues	363	177	144
Tapes for machine-readable cataloging are held locally	275	157	72

Although Table 6 seems to show that the cataloging of sets in machine-readable form has been begun but abandoned before completion in 238 instances, this is not a valid conclusion from the data. The number of holdings completely cataloged and the number for which cataloging is in-process are, as suggested above, shy of the true totals for these categories as a result of respondents' uncertainties about the status of their cataloging.

Appendix F gives sets that have been or are being cataloged on one or more bibliographic utility and Appendix G lists sets cataloged on in-house systems.

Responses to Part III: Priorities for Cataloging and Interest in Cooperative Cataloging Projects

A response grid, somewhat like Part II on a smaller scale, Part III of the survey questionnaire requests respondents to identify the microform sets that the responding library considers to be most in need of cataloging. Respondents cite sets by the same numeric identifiers used on Part II and they assign a value to each set cited on a scale of one to five, five denoting highest priority and one lowest.

In addition, Part III asks respondents to indicate whether the library would be willing to participate in a cooperative project to catalog each set that is given a priority rating.

The final question on Part III concerns the "authority" of responses. Respondents are asked to indicate whether the return represents: (1) library-wide policies or plans, (2) library-wide informal goals, (3) departmental policies or informal goals, or (4) the personal view of the respondent.

<u>Priorities for Cataloging Microform Sets</u>. The 267 libraries that returned completed copies of Part III of the survey questionnaire gave priority ratings to 466 separate sets (a total of 1,926 holdings were rated). The number of sets receiving no priority for cataloging is 343. An investigation has not yet been made to determine which, if any, of the sets that did not receive priority for cataloging would have received priority had they not already been fully cataloged.

The highest rating total (sum of all ratings) given any set is 224. The average rating per set totals 11.8, and the median rating is 6. Some libraries gave priority ratings for large numbers of sets. One gave ratings for 114 sets. Most rated only one or two. The vast majority gave priorities only for sets already owned; a few also listed ones that were being considered for purchase.

The following table summarizes priority ratings given in response to Part III. Though not generally very meaningful, the even distribution of totals given on this table does indicate that respondents gave careful thought to the relative need for cataloging each set they listed.

Table 7, Summary of Priorities For Cataloging Microform Sets

	Holdings	Sets	Libraries
Highest priority (5)	536	202	180
Next highest (4)	374	172	134
Mid-range (3)	389	231	141
Low (2)	249	154	94
Lowest (1)	323	174	110

<u>Interest in Cooperative Cataloging Projects</u>. A total of 121 respondents showed a commitment to one or more cooperative cataloging projects (45% of those completing this part of the questionnaire). This group of respondents identified 227 separate sets that they are willing to catalog cooperatively. The set most often cited in returns that give cooperative cataloging data received positive responses from 24 libraries. Most sets were given positive responses by only one or two libraries. Fifty-four sets were listed for cooperative cataloging by three or more libraries.

These response data are quite surprising. Many people had thought
interest in cooperative cataloging to be quite limited, involving very few
libraries and few sets. Only five libraries showed interest in cooperative
cataloging in the 1980 ISCI survey.

If the experience of the RLAC Microform Cataloging Task Force is
indicative, the Microform Project survey data are more than wishful thinking
on the part of respondents. Of the 13 libraries that are actively cataloging
American Fiction under RLAC auspices, two are so committed to cooperative
cataloging that they are participating despite the fact that they do not own
the set.

Levels of Authority of Responses to Part III. The following table
summarizes data on the authority of responses to Part III.

Table 8, Authority of Responses

	Libraries
Library-wide policies or plans	42
Library-wide informal goals	75
Dept. policies or informal goals	38
Personal view of respondent	72

This table shows that libraries' responses to questions on priorities and
cooperative cataloging have a high degree of authority. Seventy-one percent
of responses represent library or departmental policies or informal goals.

Although the table does not show it, the majority of those who stated
they were giving their personal views are department heads, usually heads of
technical services or of collection development departments.

Sets Given High Priority for Cataloging. The data in Part III of the
survey data base can be used to compile a list of sets given highest priority
for cataloging. An effective method for accomplishing this is to combine
those sets that have been given the highest priority ratings, with those that
have been rated by a significant number of libraries (regardless of the size
of the rating) and those which a significant number of libraries have shown an
interest in cooperative cataloging.

As a tool to assist in the development of cataloging projects, a tally
was made of sets meeting any of the following criteria: (1) a total priority
rating of at least 20, (2) priority ratings given by at least eight libraries,
and (3) at least three libraries have shown interest in cooperative
cataloging. A total of 85 sets meet this set of criteria. A listing of the
85 is given in Appendix H. Appendix I shows the sets in priority order.

Microform Sets in U.S. and Canadian Libraries

Data in Part II of the survey data base can be used to determine which high-priority sets have not received a significant amount of cataloging on any of the major bibliographic utilities.

Lists of sets that have not received a significant amount of cataloging on OCLC, RLIN, or UTLAS are found, respectively, as Appendices J, K, and L. Only three high-priority sets are shown to have received any cataloging on WLN: HRAF Microfiles (10% cataloged in an on-going program), Microfiche of Books Listed in LAW BOOKS RECOMMENDED FOR LIBRARIES (some cataloging is shown), and State Constitutional Conventions, Commissions, and Amendments on Microfiche (a very small amount cataloged).

Libraries that wish further information on the sets listed in Appendices J, K, and L should contact the project office. These sets are clearly prime candidates for any of the following actions.

The larger sets should be considered for cooperative cataloging projects. The project office can supply the names, addresses, and telephone numbers of librarians that have shown an interest in cooperative projects for each of them. Since a number of large sets are already being cataloged by individual libraries, such stand-alone cataloging is clearly also an option. The cataloging of smaller sets can be accomplished fairly easily by individual libraries. Both large and small sets are candidates for cataloging under HEA Title II-C or other grants.

The project office can assist libraries in undertaking projects such as these by providing information on libraries that are already cataloging sets as well as on those that are interested in cataloging them. It can give guidance on techniques for establishing cooperative cataloging projects, can give support for grant applications, and can put library staff in contact with OCLC personnel so that existing and newly-created records can be coded for set-processing (or profile-matching). It can also assist by putting library staff in contact with publishers as and if necessary.

As explained above, the project office can also provide information from any of the 16 categories of data in the survey data base on any of the 809 sets for which data exist. A list of sets is found as Appendix D.

Respondents' Comments on Microform Cataloging

All three parts of the survey questionnaire contained space which libraries used to comment on their responses. In addition, a number of libraries enclosed notes and letters with their response forms.

Both general and specific comments were received. The most common type of general comment is one that states simply that the task of filling out the questionnaire was difficult but useful. Many libraries had not previously inventoried their holdings of microform sets and very few had maintained detailed records concerning the bibliographic control provided for them. The great majority of these libraries were glad to have the occasion for creating such records. Other general common comments give support to the Microform Project and offer assistance, usually through participation in cataloging projects.

Respondents in libraries that hold very few sets and that are not planning to acquire new ones sometimes inserted comments saying that the Microform Project really does not apply to them.

Almost all the comments given in response to the second part of the survey concern specific holdings. Most of them specify the parts of a set that is held where they have not been able to supply the approximate percentage as requested. Others specify the parts that have been cataloged and the machine-readable records that have been created where these data cannot be given by percentages. Respondents also used Part II comments to indicate uncertainties regarding specific responses and provide clues for correcting estimating errors they may have made. A number of them give information on planned cataloging projects and on retrospective conversion programs that are planned or underway.

Appendix M contains a sampling of general statements made in both letters and comments to the first and third parts of the survey. The collection is not intended to be representative, but rather to show some of the more interesting of those that were received.

Conclusion

The Microform Project was established to assist libraries, microform publishers and the bibliographic utilities in their efforts to achieve bibliographic access to titles in microform sets. The primary tool in providing this assistance is a Microform Cataloging Clearinghouse. The main purposes of the clearinghouse are to facilitate the cataloging of titles in microform sets and prevent duplication of effort.

The clearinghouse is based on a survey sent to participants in the four major bibliographic utilities as well as the few major libraries that do not participate in them. A total of 535 useful survey returns were received. These returns show that a large number of libraries catalog titles in microform sets and that most of them create machine-readable records for at least some of the sets they catalog. The number of cataloged sets is large and appears to be growing quickly. Although many sets have nonetheless not yet received cataloging, there is reason to believe that most, perhaps all of them will be cataloged during the next few years.

The clearinghouse can help libraries by providing information on records that are already available for titles in sets that they wish to catalog; it can assist them in locating sets that have been coded for set processing, or profile matching; and it can provide information useful in preparing cataloging grant applications.

Microform Sets in U.S. and Canadian Libraries

Your help is needed in extending the clearinghouse data base: please give the project office information to update the survey responses sent in 1982. If your library has begun cataloging one or more microform sets in the past 12 to 18 months, insofar as you can, give the following data:

Set title and publisher; whether you hold the entire set, hold part and are not still receiving, or hold part and still receive segments; whether you have prepared any finding tools apart from cataloging records for titles in the set; whether you have cataloged all the titles in the set or only a portion of the titles (give percentage if you can); whether cataloging continues. Give the main source of copy, the main cataloging code observed, and the level of cataloging; state whether any records for titles in the set have been entered into a machine-readable data base and, if so, approximately what percentage; indicate whether entering of records continues; specify the data base (or data bases) into which records have been entered.

In addition, if your library has completed cataloging a set in the past 12 to 18 months, please send set title, publisher, and four-digit code (if known) to the project office. Finally, if your library has not yet sent any survey data, the project coordinator will be glad to supply a complete set of forms. Please call or write.

Jeffrey Heynen, Coordinator
ARL Microform Project
503 11th Street, SE
Washington, DC 20003
(202) 544-0291

Appendix A

Libraries Represented in the Clearinghouse Data Base

The libraries in this list all responded to Part I and at least one other Part of the Microform Project Survey.

The list is in alphabetical order by institution and library. Although most entries are shown as given on survey response forms, some have been revised so that libraries which have the same institutional affiliation (e.g. the University of California) are grouped together.

Certain libraries, such as state and public libraries, are institutions in their own right, of course. These are identified simply by institution name. All others, the majority of respondents, are connected with academic institutions or other parent organizations. These are identified first by institution, then by library name. Where respondents did not give a distinctive name, the word "library" usually, but not always, appears.

Not all insitutions and institution/library combinations are distinctive or fully recognizable. No cross-references are included in this list. However NUC symbols are provided for each entry (in parentheses) as an aid to recognition. In addition, since NUC symbols are for the most part assigned in accordance with a logical, geographical scheme, they can be used as a kind of index. For this reason an NUC symbol list of respondents is given as Appendix B.

Note that the Library of Congress publication <u>Symbols of American Libraries</u> contains an index, and can thus be used as a guide to this appendix.

Agriculture Canada, Libraries Division (CaOOAg)
Alberta Environmental Centre (CaAVeE)
Ambassador College, Library (CPA)
American Antiquarian Society, Library (MWA)
American Philosophical Society Library (PPAmP)
American University, Washington College of Law Library (DAU-L)
American University, University Library (DAU)
Amherst College, Amherst College Library (MA)
Anchorage Municipal Libraries, S.J. Loussac Public Library (AkAP)
Andrews University, James White Library (MiBsA)
Appalachian State University, Belk Library (NcBoA)
Arizona State University, University Libraries (AzTeS)
Armstrong St. College, Lane Library (GSA)
Art Institute of Chicago, Ryerson and Burnham Libraries (ICA)
Asbury College, Morrison-Kenyon Library (KyWA)
Baker University, Collins Library (KBB)
Barry University, Monsignor William Barry Memorial Library (FNmB)
Bemidji State University, A.C. Clark Library (MnBemS)

Appendix A - Libraries Represented in the Clearinghouse Data Base

Bergen Community College (NjParB)
Bethany Nazarene College, R.T. Williams Learning Resources Ctr (OkBetC)
Bloomsburg State College, Andruss Library (PBBS)
Boise State University, The Library (IdBB)
Boston College, Bapst Library (MCLB)
Boston Public Library (MB)
Boston University, Mugar Memorial Library (MBU)
Brandeis University, Library (MWalB)
Bridgewater College, Alexander Mack Memorial Library (ViBrC)
Brigham Young University, Harold B. Lee Library (UPB)
Brock University, Brock University Library (CaOStCB)
Brown University, Rockefeller Library (RPB)
California Institute of Technology, Millikan Memorial Library (CPT)
California Polytechnic State University, R.E. Kennedy Library (CSluSP)
California State College - Stanislaus, Library (CTurS)
California State College (Pennsylvania), Louis L. Manderino Library (PCalS)
California State University, Dominguez Hills, University Library (CDhS)
California State University, Fresno, Henry Madden Library (CFrS)
California State University, Fullerton, Library (CFlS)
California State University, Hayward, Library (CHS)
California State University, Long Beach, University Library (CLobS)
California State University, Northridge, University Libraries (CNoS)
California State University, Sacramento, The Library (CSS)
California Western School of Law, Library (CSdCW-L)
Calvin College and Seminary, Library (MiGrC)
Camosun College, Camosun College Library Media Centr (CaBViC)
Canada. Dept. of External Affairs (MGL) (CaOOE)
Canada. Dept. of Indian Affairs & Northern Dev., Departmental Library (CaOORD)
Carleton University (CaOOCC)
Carson-Newman College, Carson-Newman College Library (TCNC)
Case Western Reserve Univ. Libraries (OClW)
Catholic Theological Union, Library (ICTU)
Catholic University of America, Mullen Library (DCU)
Center for Reserch Libraries (ICRL)
Central Missouri State University, Ward Edwards Library (MoWarbT)
Chatham College, Jennie King Mellon Library (PPiCC)
Chattanooga Hamilton County Bicentennial Library (TC)
Claremont Colleges, Honnold Library (CCC)
Clark College, Clark College Library (WaVC)
Clarke College, Clarke Library (IaDuCl)
Clemson University, Cooper Library (SoCleU)
Cleveland State University, Cleveland-Marshall College of Law Library (OClU-L)
Clinch Valley College, John Cook Wyllie Library (ViWisC)
Colby College, Miller Library (MeWC)
College of Wiliam and Mary-Law, Marshall-Wythe Law Library (ViW-L)
College of William and Mary, Swem Library (ViW)
College of Wooster, Andrews Library (OWoC)
Colorado State University, Colorado State Univ Libraries (CoFS)
Columbia University, Butler Library (NNC)
Columbia University, Teachers College Library (NNC-T)
Community College of Allegheny County, CCAC Allegheny Campus Library (PPiAC)
Concordia College, Carl B. Ylvisaker Library (MnMohC)

Concordia College, Buenger Memorial Library (MnSC)
Concordia Teachers College, Lind Library (NbSeT)
Concordia Theological Seminary, Library (InFwCT)
Concordia University, Concordia University Libraries (CaQMG)
Connecticut College, Connecticut College Library (CtNlC)
Conoco Inc. - Coal Research Division (PLibCon)
Coppin State College, Parlett More Library (MdBCS)
Cornell University, Cornell University Libraries (NIC)
Creighton University, Alumni Memorial Library (NbOC)
Dalhousie University, Killam Library (CaNSHD)
Dartmouth College, Dartmouth College Library (NhD)
Davidson College, Davidson College Library (NcDaD)
DePaul University Law School, DePaul Law Library (ICD-L)
Douglas College, Douglas College Libraries (CaBNWD)
Drury College, Walker Library (MoSpD)
Duke University, William R. Perkins Library (NcD)
Duke University, Duke Univ. School of Law Library (NcD-L)
Duquesne University, Duquesne University Library (PPiD)
Earlham College Library (InRE)
East Carolina University, Joyner Library (NcGrE)
East Texas State University, James Gee Library (TxComS)
Eastern Michigan University, Eastern Michigan University Library (MiYEM)
Eastern New Mexico University, Golden Library (NmPE)
Eastern Washington University, JFK Library (WaChenE)
Eden-Webster Libraries (MoWgT/W)
Emory & Henry College, Frederick T. Kelly Library (ViEmoE)
Emory University, Div. of Library & Info. Mgmt. Lib. (GEU-LS)
Emory University, Pitts Theology Library (GEU-T)
Emory University, Robert W. Woodruff Library (GEU)
Energy, Mines & Resources Canada, Resource Economics Library (CaOOMR)
Enoch Pratt Free Library (MdBE)
Episcopal Divinity/Weston School Theology, The Libraries (MCE/MCW)
Evangel College, Evangel College Library (MoSpE)
Evergreen State College, Daniel J. Evans Library (WaOE)
Fairfield University, Nyselius Library (CtFaU)
Flagler College, Louise Wise Lewis Library (FSpF)
Florida Atlantic University, S.E. Wimberly Library (FBoU)
Florida International Univ.-Tamiami Camp, Library (FMFIU)
Florida State University, College of Law Library (FTaSU-L)
Florida State University, Robert Manning Strozier Library (FTaSU)
Fordham University, Fordham University Library (NNF)
Furman University, James Buchannan Duke Library (ScGF)
George Mason University, Fenurick Library (ViFGM)
George Washington University, Gelman Library (DGw)
Georgia College, The Library (GWiC)
Georgia Institute of Technology, Price Gilbert Memorial Library (GAT)
Georgia Southern College, Georgia Southern College Library (GStG)
Georgia State University, Pullen Library (GASU)
Glenville State College (WvGlS)
Gonzaga University, Crosby Library (WaSpG)
Gonzaga University, Law School Library (WaSpG-L)
Governors State University, University Library (IPfsG)

Appendix A - Libraries Represented in the Clearinghouse Data Base

Grace College and Seminary, Grace College & Seminary Library (InWinG)
Graduate Theological Union, Graduate Theological Union Library (CBGTU)
Hamilton College, Burke Library (NCH)
Hamilton Public Library (CaOH)
Hamline University School of Law, Law Library (MnSH-L)
Harvard University, Harvard College Library (MH)
Harvard University, Fine Arts Library (MH-FA)
Harvard University, Harvard Law Library (MH-L)
Harvard University - Peabody Museum, Tozzer Library (MH-P)
Hebrew Union Coll.-Jewish Inst. of Rel., Klau Library (OCH)
Henry F. du Pont Winterthur Museum, Joseph Downs Manuscript & Microfilm (DeWint)
Herbert H. Lehman College, Library (NNL)
Herkimer County Community College (NIlH)
Historical Society of Pennsylvania (PHi)
Hobbs Public Library (NmHo)
Hofstra University, Hofstra University Library (NHemH)
Houston Public Library (TxH)
Howard University, Howard University Libraries (DHU)
Humboldt State University, Library (CArcHT)
Huntington Library, Huntington Library (CSmH)
Illinois Agricultural Association, IAA & Affiliated Companies Library (IBloIAA)
Illinois State University, Milner Library (INS)
Indiana State University, Cunningham Memorial Library (InTI)
Indiana University, Indiana University Libraries (InU)
Indiana University Medical Center, Wishard Mem. Hosp. Professional Lib (InU-MC)
Institute for Advanced Study of World Religion, Library (NSbIA)
Institute of Gas Technology, Technical Information Center (ICI-G)
Iowa State University, Iowa State University Library (IaAS)
Jacksonville State University, University Library (AJacT)
James Madison University, Madison Memorial Library (ViHart)
Johns Hopkins University, Eisenhower Library (MdBJ)
Kansas State Library (K)
Kansas State University, Kansas State University Liraries (KMK)
Kearney State College, Calvin T. Ryan Library (NbKS)
Kennesaw College, Kennesaw College Library (GMark)
Kent State Universty, Kent State University Libraries (OKentC)
Knoxville-Knox County Public Library, Lawson McGhee Library (TKL)
Kutztown State College, Rohrbach Library (PKuS)
LaGrange College, Banks Library (GLagC)
Lamar University, Mary & John Gray Library (TxBeaL)
Laredo State University, Harold R. Yeary Library (TxLarU)
Lawrence University, Seeley G. Mudd Library (WAL)
Lee College, Lee Memorial Library (TCleL)
Lehigh University, Lehigh University Libraries (PBL)
Library Company of Philadelphia (PPL)
Library of Congress (DLC)
Linda Hall Library (MoKL)
Lindenwood Colleges, M.L. Butler Library (MoStcL)
Livermore Public Library (CLiv)
Loch Haven State College, Stevenson Library (PLhS)
Lorain Public Library (OLor)
Los Angeles County Museum of Art, Art Research Library (CLCMAT)

Appendix A - Libraries Represented in the Clearinghouse Data Base

Los Angeles County Public Library (CLCo)
Louisiana State Library (L)
Louisiana State University, Troy H. Middleton Library (LU)
Louisiana State University, Hebert Law Center Library (LU-L)
Louisville Free Public Library (KyLo)
Loyola University - Law School, Law Library (LNL-L)
Loyola/Notre Dame Library, Inc. (MdBLN)
Lycoming College (PWmL)
Macalester College, Weyerhaeuser Library (MnSM)
Manhattan College, Cardinal Hayes Library (NNMan)
Manitoba Dept. of Education (CaMWE)
Mansfield-Richland County Public Library (OMans)
Maryville College (MoSMa)
Massachusetts Institute of Technology, M.I.T. Libraries (MCM)
May Department Stores Company, Corporate Information Center (May)
Mayo Clinic, Library (MnRM)
McGill University, McLennan Library (CaQMM)
McMaster University, Mills Memorial Library (CaOHM)
Medical College of Wisconsin, Todd Wehr Library (WMMCW)
Memorial University of Newfoundland, Queen Elizabeth II Library (CaNfSM)
Memphis State University, University Libraries (TMM)
Mercer University, Walter F. George School of Law Lib. (GMM-L)
Metropolitan Technical Community College, Library (NbOMC)
Miami University, Edgar W. King Library (OOxM)
Michigan State University, Libraries (MiEM)
Middle Georgia College, Roberts Memorial Library (GCocM)
Middlebury College, Starr Library (VtMiM)
Midland Lutheran College, Luther Library (NbFrM)
Mine Safety & Health Administration, MSHA Library (CoDMSH)
Ministere Des Communications, Bibliotheque Administrative (CaQQCo)
Mississippi College - School of Law, Law Library (MsJMCL)
Mississippi Library Commission (MsLC)
Montana State University, Renne Library (MtBC)
Moraine Valley Community College, Learning Resources Center (IPhiM)
Morehead State University, Camden-Carroll Library (KyMoreU)
Mount Allison University, Ralph Pickard Bell Library (CaNBSaM)
Mount Angel Abbey, Mount Angel Abbey Library (OrStbM)
Muhlenberg College, Muhlenberg-Cedar Crest Libraries (PAtM)
Murray State University, Waterfield Library (KyMurt)
Museum of Fine Arts, Boston (MBMu)
National Agricultural Library - USDA (DNAL)
National Gallery of Canada, National Gallery Library (CaOONG)
National Library of Canada (CaOONL)
National Library of Medicine (DNLM)
National Museums of Canada-Library Services (CaOONM)
Canada Institute for Scientific and Technical Information (CaOON)
Nazareth College Of Rochester, Lorette Wilmot Library (NRNC)
Nebraska Library Commission (Nb-LC)
New Castle Public Library (PNc)
New Mexico Tech., Martin Speare Memorial Library (NmSoI)
New York Law School Library (NNLS)
New York Public Library, Research Libraries (NN)

New York State Library (N)
New York University, Bobst Library (NNU)
Newport Beach Public Library (CNb)
North Carolina Central University, School of Library Science (NcDurCLS)
North Carolina State University, D. H. Hill Library (NcRS)
North Dakota State University, The Library (NdFA)
North Texas State University, University Libraries (TxDN)
Northeastern Illinois University (ICNE)
Northeastern University, Dodge Library (MBNU)
Northern Illinois University, NIU Libraries (IDeKN)
Northern Illinois University, College of Law Library (IDeKN-L)
Northern Kentucky University, W. Frank Steely Library (KyHhN)
Northern Michigan University, Olson Library (MiMarqN)
Northern Montana College, Library (MtHaN)
Northern State College, Williams Library (SdAbN)
Northwest Nazarene College, Riley Library (IdNN)
Northwestern University, Northwestern University Library (IEN)
Oglethorpe University (GAOC)
Ohio Northern University, Heterick Memorial Library (OAdN)
Ohio State Library, State Library of Ohio (O)
Ohio State University, Main Library (OU)
Ohio State University, Edgar Dale Media Center (OU-ED)
Ohio University, Ohio University Library (OAU)
Ohio University - Lancaster, Library (OLanU)
Oklahoma City University, Law Library (OkOkU-L)
Oklahoma State University, Library (OkS)
Olivet College, Burrage Library (MiOC)
Oral Roberts University, Oral Roberts University Library (OkTOR)
Orange County Law Library (COrCL)
Oregon State University, Oregon State University Library (OrCS)
Orlando Public Library (FO)
Pacific Christian College, Hurst Memorial Library (CFP)
Pacific Lutheran University, Mortvedt Library (WaPIP)
Pan American University, Learning Resource Center (TxEdP)
Peabody Institute of the Johns Hopkins U, Peabody Conservatory Library (MdBP)
Pekin Community High School, East Campus (IPeKC)
Pennsylvania State Univ. Capitol Campus, Heindel Library (PSt-Ca)
Pennsylvania State University, Pattee Library (PSt)
Philadelphia College of Textiles & Sci, Pastore Library (PPPTe)
Pittsburg State University, Leonard H. Axe Library (KPT)
Plymouth State College, Lamson Library (NhPlS)
Point Park College, Helen Sean Moore Library (PPiPP)
Polytechnic Institute of New York, Library (NBPol)
Porter Public Library (OWest)
Princeton Theological Seminary, Speer Library (NjPT)
Princeton University, Princeton University Library (NjP)
Providence College, Phillips Memorial Library (RPPC)
Public Library of Charlotte/Mecklenburg (NcC)
Purdue University, Calumet Library (InHamP)
Queen's University, Douglas Library (CaOKQ)
Queens College, Queens College Library (NFQ)
Ramsey County Public Library (MnSRC)

Rhode Island Historical Society, Library (RHi)
Rice University, Fondren Library (TxHR)
Rochester Institute of Technology, Wallace Memorial Library (NRRI)
Roger Williams College, Library (RBrRW)
Rosary College, Rebecca Crown Library (IRivfR)
Rosemont College, Gertrude Kistler Memorial Library (PRosC)
Rutgers University, Alexander Library (NjR)
SUNY College at Brockport, Drake Memorial Library (NBrockU)
SUNY College at Cortland, Memorial Library (NCortU)
SUNY College at Old Westbury, Library (NOwU)
SUNY College at Oneonta, J.M. Milne Library (NOneoU)
SUNY College at Purchase, Library (NPurU)
SUNY College of Technology at Utica/Rome, Library (NUtSU)
SUNY at Albany, University Libraries (NAlU)
SUNY at Binghamton, Glenn G. Bartle Library (NBiSU)
SUNY at Buffalo, Library (NBuU)
SUNY at Buffalo - Law Library (NBuU-L)
SUNY at Potsdam, F.W.Crumb Memorial Library (NPotU)
SUNY at Stony Brook, Melville Library (NSbSU)
San Antonio College, Library (TxSaC)
San Diego State University, University Library (CSdS)
San Francisco State University, Leonard Library (CSfSt)
Saskatchewan Provincial Library (CaSRP)
Secretary of State-Translation Bureau, Documentation Directorate (CaOOSST)
Shippensburg State College, Ezra Lehman Memorial Library (PShS)
Simmons College, Beatley Library (MBSi)
Sioux Falls College, Norman B. Mears Library (SdSifC)
Skyline College, Skyline College Library (CSbrSC)
Smith College, Library (MNS)
Smithsonian Institution, Smithsonian Institution Libraries (DSI)
South Dakota Sch. of Mines & Technology, Devereaux Library (SdRM)
South Dakota State Library (Sd)
South Dakota State University, Hilton M. Briggs Library (SdB)
Southeast Missouri State University, Kent Library (MoCgS)
Southeastern Baptist Theological Seminary (NcWfSB)
Southern California Rapid Transit District (SLSC)
Southern Illinois University - Carbondale, Morris Library (ICarbS)
Southern Illinois University - Edwardsville, Lovejoy Library (IEdS-E)
Southern Methodist University, Central University Libraries (TxDaM)
Southern Methodist University, Bridwell Library-Perkins School (TxDaM-P)
Southern University & A&M College, Southern University Library (LScS)
Southern Utah State College (UCS)
St. Anselm College, Geisel Library (NhMSA)
St. John's University, Alcuin Library (MnSC)
St. Joseph's University, Drexel Library (PPSJ)
St. Lawrence University, Owen D. Young Library (NCaS)
St. Louis University, Omar Poos Law Library (MoSU-L)
St. Louis University, Pius XII Memorial Library (MoSU)
St. Paul Public Library (MnS)
St. Vincent College, St. Vincent College Library (PLatS)
Stanford University, Green Library (CSt)
Starved Rock Library System (IOtS)

State Historical Society of Wisconsin, Library (WHi)
State University College at Fredonia (NY), Reed Library (NFredU)
State University College at Buffalo (NY), E. H. Butler Library (NBuC)
State University College at Oswego (NY), Penfield Library (NOsU)
Supreme Court at Syracuse, Library (NSySC)
Susquehanna University, Roger M. Blough Learning Center (PSelS)
Swarthmore College, Friends Historical Library (PSC-Hi)
Swarthwore College, McCabe Library (PSC)
Syracuse University, Syracuse University Libraries (NSyU)
Temple University, Samuel Paley Library (PPT)
Texas A & M University, Sterling C. Evans Library (TxCM)
Texas A & M University at Galveston (TxGML)
Texas Christian University, Mary Couts Burnett Library (TxFTC)
Texas Tech University, Texas Tech University Library (TxLT)
Texas Tech University - Law School, School of Law Library (TxLT-L)
Texas Woman's University, Texas Woman's University Library (TxDW)
Toronto Board of Education, Reference Section, Educ. Centre Lib (CaOTEC)
Transylvania University, Frances Carrick Thomas Library (KyLxT)
Trenton State College, West Library (NjTS)
Trinity University, Library (TxSaT)
Tucson Public Library, Tucson Public Library (AzT)
Tufts University, Tufts University Library (MMeT)
Tufts University, Fletcher School, Ginn Library (MMeT-F)
U.S. Army Engineer District, Louisville, Corps of Engineers - Library (KyLoACE)
U.S. Army War College, U.S. Army War College Library (PCarlA)
U.S. Coast Guard Academy, U.S. Coast Guard Academy (CtNlCG)
U.S. Court House, Judges' Library, Rm. 5518 (DUCA)
U.S. Dept. of Energy, Energy Library (DERDA)
U.S. Dept. of Justice, Justice Main Library (DJ)
U.S. Dept. of the Interior, U.S. Geological Survey (DI-GS)
U.S. Dept. of the Treasury, Room 5310, Main Treasury Bldg. (DT)
U.S. Environmental Protection Agency, Library (OCEPA)
U.S. Military Academy, Library (NWM)
U.S. Naval Academy, Nimitz Library (MdAN)
Union College, Schaffer Library (NSchU)
Universite Laval, Bibliotheque (CaQQLa)
Universite de Moncton, Bibliotheque Champlain (CaNBMoU)
Universite de Montreal, Service des bibliotheques (CaQMU)
Universite de Sherbrooke, Bibliotheque generale (CaQSherU)
University of Akron, Beirce Library (OAkU)
University of Alabama, University of Alabama Library (AU)
University of Alabama in Birmingham, Mervyn Sterne Library (ABAU)
University of Alberta, University Library (CaAEU)
University of Arizona, Library (AzU)
University of Arkansas, University of Arkansas Libraries (ArU)
University of Bridgeport, Magnus Wahlstrom Library (CtBU)
University of British Columbia, Library (CaBVaU)
University of California - Berkeley, Institute of Transportation Studies (CUIT)
University of California - Berkeley, Main Library (CU)
University of California - Davis, The General Library (CU-A)
University of California - Davis, Health Sciences Library (CU-AM)
University of California - Irvine, Library (CU-I)

Appendix A - Libraries Represented in the Clearinghouse Data Base

University of California - Riverside, The General Library (CU-Riv)
University of California - San Diego, Central University Library (CU-S)
University of California - San Francisco, The Library (CUM)
University of California - Santa Barbara, Library (CU-SB)
University of Caifornia - Santa Cruz, University Library (CU-SC)
University of Cincinnati, Central Library (OCU)
University of Colorado - Boulder, Univ. of Colorado Boulder Libraries (CoU)
University of Colorado at Denver, Auraria Library (CoU-DA)
University of Connecticut, University of Connecticut Library (CtU)
University of Dallas, Main Library (TxDaU)
University of Dayton, Roesch Library (ODaU)
University of Denver, Penrose Library (CoDU)
University of Detroit, library (MiDU)
University of Georgia, University of Georgia Libraries (GU)
University of Hawaii at Manoa, Hamilton Library (HU)
University of Houston - Clear Lake City, Library and Learning Resources (TxClcU)
University of Idaho, Library (IdU)
University of Illinois - Chicago Circle, Library (ICIU)
University of Illinois - Medical Center, Library of the Health Sciences (IU-M)
University of Illinois - Urbana, Library - Room 246 (IU)
University of Iowa, University Libraries (IaU)
University of Iowa, Law Library (IaU-L)
University of Kansas, Watson Library (KU)
University of Kansas Medical Center, Clendening Library (KU-M)
University of Kansas-Law, Law Library (KU-L)
University of Kentucky, Libraries (KyU)
University of Louisville, Ekstrom Library (KyLou)
University of Maine, Fogler Library (MeU)
University of Manitoba, Dafoe Library (CaMWU)
University of Mary Hardin-Baylor, Townsend Memorial Library (TxBelM)
University of Maryland, Health Sciences Library (MdU-H)
University of Maryland, College Park, McKeldin Library (MdU)
University of Massachusetts/Amherst, University Library (MU)
University of Miami, Library (FMU)
University of Michigan - Ann Arbor, University Library (MiU)
University of Minnesota, Wilson Library (MnU)
University of Minnesota-Law, Law Library (MnU-L)
University of Mississippi, John Davis Williams Library (MsU)
University of Mississippi, Law School Library (MsU-L)
University of Missouri-Columbia, Ellis Library (MoU)
University of Missouri-Kansas City, Libraries (MoKU)
University of Montana, Mansfield Library (MtU)
University of Nebraska-Lincoln, Libraries (NbU)
University of New Brunswick, Harriet Irving Library (CaNBFU)
University of New Hampshire, Dimond Library (NhU)
University of New Mexico, General Library (NmU)
University of New Orleans, Earl K. Long Library (LNU)
University of North Carolina (Chapel Hill), Wilson Library (NcU)
University of North Carolina-Asheville, Ramsey Library (NcAU)
University of North Carolina-Greensboro, Jackson Library (NcGU)
University of North Carolina-Chapel Hill, Health Sciences Library (NcU-H)
University of North Carolina-Charlotte, J. Murrey Atkins Library (NcCU)

University of North Dakota, Chester Fritz Library (NdU)
University of Northern Colorado, James A. Michener Library (CoGrU)
University of Notre Dame, University Libraries (InNd)
University of Oklahoma, University of Oklahoma Libraries (OkU)
University of Oklahoma Law Center, O.U. Law Center Library (OkU-L)
University of Oregon, Library (OrU)
University of Ottawa, Morisset Library (CaOOU)
University of Pennsylvania, Van Pelt Library CH (PU)
University of Pittsburgh, Hillman Library (PPiU)
University of Puget Sound, Univ. of Puget Sound-Law Library (WaTU-L)
University of Redlands, Armacost Library (CRedlU)
University of Rhode Island, University Library (RU)
University of Rochester, Library (NRU)
University of Santa Clara, Michel Orradre Library (CStclU)
University of Saskatchewan, Library (CaSSU)
University of Scranton, Alumni Memorial Library (PScU)
University of South Alabama, Library (AMobU)
University of South Carolina, Thomas Cooper Library (ScU)
University of South Carolina, Law Library (ScU-L)
University of South Florida, Library (FTS)
University of South Florida - St. Petersburg, Poynter Library (FSpU*)
University of Southern California, Doheny Library (CLSU)
University of Southern Mississippi, Cook Library (MsHaU)
University of Tampa, Merl Kelce Library (FTU)
University of Tennessee, James D. Hoskins Library (TU)
University of Tennessee at Martin, Paul Meek Library (TMaU)
University of Texas at Arlington, UTA Library (TxArU)
University of Texas at Austin, General Libraries (TxU)
University of Texas at Dallas, McDermott Library (TxU-Da)
University of Texas at El Paso, Library - Serials (TxEU)
University of Texas at San Antonio, Library (TxSaU)
University of Toledo College of Law, College of Law Library (OTU-L)
University of Toronto, Library (CaOTU)
University of Tulsa, McFarlin Library (OkTU)
University of Utah, University Libraries (UU)
University of Vermont, Bailey/Howe Library (VtU)
University of Victoria, McPherson Library (CaBViU)
University of Virginia, Alderman Library (ViU)
University of Virginia-Law, Law Library (ViU-L)
University of Washington, University of Washington Libraries (WaU)
University of Waterloo, Arts Library (CaOWtU)
University of Western Ontario, D.B. Weldon Library (CaOLU)
University of Wisconsin-Eau Claire, McIntyre Library (WEU)
University of Wisconsin-Green Bay, Library Learning Center (WGrU)
University of Wisconsin-La Crosse, Murphy Library (WLacU)
University of Wisconsin-Madison, Law Library (WU-L)
University of Wisconsin-Madison, Memorial Library (WU)
University of Wisconsin-Madison, Middleton Health Sciences Library (WU-M)
University of Wisconsin-Milwaukee, Golda Meir Library (WMUW)
University of Wisconsin-Parkside, Library/Learning Center (WKenU)
University of Wisconsin-River Falls, Chalmer Davee Library (WRFC)
University of Wisconsin-Stevens Point, Learning Resources Center (WSpU)

University of Wisconsin-Stout, Library Learning Center (WMenU)
University of Wisconsin-Whitewater, Harold Andersen Library (WWhiwU)
University of Wyoming, University of Wyoming Library (WyU)
Upper Arlington Public Library (OUa)
Valdosta State College, Valdosta State College Library (GVaS)
Valparaiso University, Moellering Library (InValU)
Vancouver Community College, Langara Library (CaBVaVC)
Vanderbilt University, Vanderbilt University Library (TNJ)
Victoria University, Victoria University Library (CaOTV)
Virginia Polytechnic Inst & State Univ, Libraries (ViBlbV)
Virginia State University, Johnston Memorial Library (ViPetS)
Wabash College, Lilly Library (InCW)
Wake Forest University, Z. Smith Reynolds Library (NcWsW)
Washington State University, Holland Library (WaPS)
Washington University in St. Louis, University Libraries (MoSW)
Wayne State University, Purdy Library (MiDW)
Wayne State University-Medical School, Shiffman Medical Library (MiDW-M)
Weber State College, Steward Library (UOW)
Wellesley College, Wellesley College Library (MWelC)
Wentworth Institute of Technology, Library (MBWI)
Wesleyan University, OLIN Library (CtW)
West Chester State College, Francis Harvey Green Library (PWcT)
West Georgia College, Irvine S. Ingram Library (GCarrWG)
West Texas State University, Cornette Library (TxCaW)
West Virginia College of Graduate Study, Library (WvICG)
West Virginia University, West Virginia University Library (WvU)
Westchester Community College, Learning Resource Center (NValhW)
Western Carolina University, Hunter Library (NcCuW)
Western Connecticut State College, Ruth A. Haas Library (CtDabN)
Western Illinois University, Library (IMacoW)
Western Michigan University, Waldo Library (MiKW)
Western Montana College, Lucy Carson Memorial Library (MtDiW)
Western New England College, Churchill Library (MSWNEC)
Western New Mexico University, Miller Library (NmScW)
Western State College, Savage Library (CoGuW)
Whittier College, Wardman Library (CWhC)
Whitworth College Library (WaSpW)
Wichita State University, Library/Medical Resources Center (KWiU)
Wilkes College, Eugene Shedden Farley Library (PWbW)
Willard Library of Evansville (InEW)
William Paterson College of New Jersey, Sarah Burd Askew Library (NjWP)
Winthrop College, Winthrop College Library (ScRhW)
Wittenberg University, Thomas Library (OSW)
Wright State University, University Library (ODaWU)
Xavier University, MacDonald Library (OCX)
Xavier University Library (LNX)
Yale University, Yale University Library (CtY)
York University, York University Libraries (CaOTY)
York University, York University Law Library (CaOTYL)
Youngstown State University, Maag Library (OYU)

Appendix B

NUC Symbol List for Libraries that Responded to Part I
and at Least One Other Part of the Survey Questionnaire

The list was drawn from the same data base as that in Appendix A and the introductory comments given there regarding institutions and libraries apply here as well. Because the list is presented in order by NUC symbol, there is no major advantage in regularizing insitution and library names. For that reason they appear in the list with abbreviations and inconsistent punctuation as the appear in the clearinghouse data base.

The Library of Congress publication _Symbols_ _of_ _American_ _Libraries_ gives a listing of libraries by NUC symbol and thus may be used as a source of further information on libraries listed here.

NUC Symbol	Institution & Library
ABAU	University of Alabama in Birmingham, Mervyn Sterne Library
AJacT	Jacksonville State University, University Library
AMobU	University of South Alabama, Library
AU	University of Alabama, University of Alabama Library
AkAP	Anchorage Municipal Libraries, S.J. Loussac Public Library
ArU	University of Arkansas, University of Arkansas Libraries
AzT	Tucson Public Library, Tucson Public Library
AzTeS	Arizona State University, University Libraries
AzU	University of Arizona, Library
CArcHT	Humboldt State University, Library
CBGTU	Graduate Theological Union, Graduate Theological Union Library
CCC	Claremont Colleges, Honnold Library
CDhS	California State Univ. Dominguez Hills, University Library
CFP	Pacific Christian College, Hurst Memorial Library
CFlS	California State University, Fullerton, Library
CFrS	California State University, Fresno, Henry Madden Library
CHS	California State University-Hayward, Library
CLCMAT	Los Angeles County Museum of Art, Art Research Library
CLCo	Los Angeles County Public Library
CLSU	University of Southern California, Doheny Library
CLiv	Livermore Public Library
CLobS	California State Univ. Long Beach, University Library
CNb	Newport Beach Public Library
CNoS	California State University - Northridge, University Libraries
COrCL	Orange County Law Library
CPA	Ambassador College, Library

CPT	California Institute of Technology, Millikan Memorial Library
CRedlU	University of Redlands, Armacost Library
CSS	California State University, Sacramento, The Library
CSbrSC	Skyline College, Skyline College Library
CSdCW-L	California Western School of Law, Library
CSdS	San Diego State University, University Library
CSfSt	San Francisco State University, Leonard Library
CSluSP	Calif. Polytechnic State University, R.E. Kennedy Library
CSmH	Huntington Library, Huntington Library
CSt	Stanford University, Green Library
CStclU	University of Santa Clara, Michel Orradre Library
CTurS	California State Coll. - Stanislaus, Library
CU	University of California - Berkeley, Main Library
CU-A	University of California - Davis, The General Library
CU-AM	University of California, Davis, Health Sciences Library
CU-I	University of California - Irvine, Library
CU-Riv	University of California, Riverside, The General Library
CU-S	University of California - San Diego, Central University Library
CU-SB	University of California, Santa Barbara, Library
CU-SC	University of Caifornia- Santa Cruz, University Library
CUIT	Inst. of Trans. Studies/Univ.California, Library
CUM	University of California-San Francisco, The Library
CWhC	Whittier College, Wardman Library
CaAEU	University of Alberta, University Library
CaAVeE	Alberta Environmental Centre
CaBNWD	Douglas College, Douglas College Libraries
CaBVaU	University of British Columbia, Univ. of British Columbia Library
CaBVaVC	Vancouver Community College, Langara Library
CaBViC	Camosun College, Camosun College Library Media Centr
CaBViV	University of Victoria, McPherson Library
CaMWE	Manitoba Dept. of Education
CaMWU	University of Manitoba, Dafoe Library
CaNBFU	University of New Brunswick, Harriet Irving Library
CaNBMoU	Universite de Moncton, Bibliotheque Champlain
CaNBSaM	Mount Allison University, Ralph Pickard Bell Library
CaNSHD	Dalhousie University, Killam Library
CaNfSM	Memorial University of Newfoundland, Queen Elizabeth II Library
CaOH	Hamilton Public Library
CaOHM	McMaster University, Mills Memorial Library
CaOKQ	Queen's University, Douglas Library
CaOLU	University of Western Ontario, D.B. Weldon Library
CaOOAg	Agriculture Canada, Libraries Division
CaOOCC	Carleton University, Library
CaOOE	Dept. of External Affairs (MGL),
CaOOMR	Energy, Mines & Resources Canada, Resource Economics Library
CaOON	National Research Council of Canada, Canada Inst. for Sci.& Tech. Inform
CaOONG	National Gallery of Canada, National Gallery Library
CaOONL	National Library of Canada
CaOONM	National Museums of Canada-Library Servs
CaOORD	Dept. of Indian Affairs & Northern Dev., Departmental Library
CaOOSST	Secretary of State-Translation Bureau, Documentation Directorate
CaOOU	University of Ottawa, Morisset Library

CaOStCB	Brock University, Brock University Library
CaOTEC	Toronto Board of Education, Reference Section, Educ. Centre Lib
CaOTU	University of Toronto, Library
CaOTV	Victoria University, Victoria University Library
CaOTY	York University, York University Libraries
CaOTYL	York University, York University Law Library
CaOWtU	University of Waterloo, Arts Library
CaQMG	Concordia University, Concordia University Libraries
CaQMM	McGill University, McLennan Library
CaQMU	Universite de Montreal, Service des bibliotheques
CaQQCo	Ministere Des Communications, Bibliotheque Administrative
CaQQLa	Universite Laval, Bibliotheque
CaQSherU	Universite de Sherbrooke, Bibliotheque generale
CaSRP	Saskatchewan Provincial Library
CaSSU	University of Saskatchewan, Library
CoDMSH	Mine Safety & Health Administration, MSHA Library
CoDU	University of Denver, Penrose Library
CoFS	Colorado State University, Colorado State Univ Libraries
CoGrU	University of Northern Colorado, James A. Michener Library
CoGuW	Western State College, Savage Library
CoU	University of Colorado - Boulder, Univ. of Colorado Boulder Libraries
CoU-DA	University of Colorado at Denver, Auraria Library
CtBU	University of Bridgeport, Magnus Wahlstrom Library
CtDabN	Western Connecticut State College, Ruth A. Haas Library
CtFaU	Fairfield University, Nyselius Library
CtNlC	Connecticut College, Connecticut College Library
CtNlCG	U.S. Coast Guard Academy, U.S. Coast Guard Academy
CtU	University of Connecticut, University of Connecticut Library
CtW	Wesleyan University, OLIN Library
CtY	Yale University, Yale University Library
DAU	American University, University Library
DAU-L	American University, Washington College of Law Library
DCU	Catholic University of America, Mullen Library
DERDA	U.S. Dept. of Energy, Energy Library
DGw	George Washington University, Gelman Library
DHU	Howard University, Howard University Libraries
DI-GS	U.S. Department of the Interior, U.S. Geological Survey
DJ	Dept. of Justice, Justice Main Library
DLC	Library of Congress
DNAL	National Agricultural Library - USDA
DNLM	National Library of Medicine
DSI	Smithsonian Institution, Smithsonian Institution Libraries
DT	U.S. Dept. of the Treasury, Library
DUCA	U.S. Court House, Judges' Library
DeWint	Henry F. du Pont Winterthur Museum, Joseph Downs Manuscript & Microfilm
FBoU	Florida Atlantic University, S.E. Wimberly Library
FMFIU	Florida International Univ.-Tamiami Camp, Library
FMU	University of Miami, Library
FNmB	Barry University, Monsignor William Barry Mem. Lib.
FO	Orlando Public Library
FSpF	Flagler College, Louise Wise Lewis Library
FSpU*	University of South Florida - St. Pete, Poynter Library

FTS	University of South Florida, Library
FTU	University of Tampa, Merl Kelce Library
FTaSU	Florida State University, Robert Manning Strozier Library
FTaSU-L	Florida State University, College of Law Library
GAOC	Oglethorpe University, Library
GASU	Georgia State University, Pullen Library
GAT	Georgia Institute of Technology, Price Gilbert Memorial Library
GCarrWG	West Georgia College, Irvine S. Ingram Library
GCocM	Middle Georgia College, Roberts Memorial Library
GEU	Emory University, Robert W. Woodruff Library
GEU-LS	Emory University, Div. of Library & Info. Mgmt. Lib.
GEU-T	Emory University, Pitts Theology Library
GLagC	LaGrange College, Banks Library
GMM-L	Mercer University, Walter F. George School of Law Lib.
GMark	Kennesaw College, Kennesaw College Library
GSA	Armstrong St. College, Lane Library
GStG	Georgia Southern College, Georgia Southern College Library
GU	University of Georgia, University of Georgia Libraries
GVaS	Valdosta State College, Valdosta State College Library
GWiC	Georgia College, The Library
HU	University of Hawaii at Manoa, Hamilton Library
IBloIAA	Illinois Agricultural Association, IAA & Affiliated Companies Library
ICA	Art Institute of Chicago, Ryerson and Burnham Libraries
ICD-L	DePaul University Law School, DePaul Law Library
ICI-G	Institute of Gas Technology, Technical Information Center
ICIU	University of Illinois - Chicago Circle, Library
ICNE	Northeastern Illinois University, Library
ICRL	Center for Reserch Libraries
ICTU	Catholic Theological Union, Library
ICarbS	Southern Illinois Univ. - Carbondale, Morris Library
IDeKN	Northern Illinois University, NIU Libraries
IDeKN-L	Northern Illinois University, College of Law Library
IEN	Northwestern University, Northwestern University Library
IEdS-E	Southern Illinois Univ.- Edwardsville, Lovejoy Library
IMacoW	Western Illinois University, Library
INS	Illinois State University, Milner Library
IOtS	Starved Rock Library System
IPeKC	Pekin Community High School, East Campus
IPfsG	Governors State University, University Library
IPhiM	Moraine Valley Community College, Learning Resources Center
IRivfR	Rosary College, Rebecca Crown Library
IU	University of Illinois - Urbana, Library - Room 246
IU-M	University of Illinois - Medical Center, Library of the Health Sciences
IaAS	Iowa State University, Iowa State University Library
IaDuCl	Clarke College, Clarke Library
IaU	University of Iowa, University Libraries
IaU-L	University of Iowa, Law Library
IdBB	Boise State University, The Library
IdNN	Northwest Nazarene College, Riley Library
IdU	University of Idaho, Library
InCW	Wabash College, Lilly Library
InEW	Willard Library of Evansville

InFwCT	Concordia Theological Seminary, Library
InHamP	Purdue University, Calumet Library
InNd	University of Notre Dame, University Libraries
InRE	Earlham College Library
InTI	Indiana State University, Cunningham Memorial Library
InU	Indiana University, Indiana University Libraries
InU-MC	Indiana Univ. Medical Center, Wishard Mem. Hosp. Professional Lib
InValU	Valparaiso University, Moellering Library
InWinG	Grace College and Seminary, Grace College & Seminary Library
K	Kansas State Library
KBB	Baker University, Collins Library
KMK	Kansas State University, Kansas State University Liraries
KPT	Pittsburg State University, Leonard H. Axe Library
KU	University of Kansas, Watson Library
KU-L	University of Kansas-Law, Law Library
KU-M	University of Kansas Medical Center, Clendening Library
KWiU	Wichita State University, Library/Medical Resources Center
KyHhN	Northern Kentucky University, W. Frank Steely Library
KyLo	Louisville Free Public Library
KyLoACE	U.S. Army Engineer District, Louisville, Corps of Engineers - Library
KyLou	University of Louisville, Ekstrom Library
KyLxT	Transylvania University, Frances Carrick Thomas Library
KyMoreU	Morehead State University, Camden-Carroll Library
KyMurt	Murray State University, Waterfield Library
KyU	University of Kentucky, Libraries
KyWA	Asbury College, Morrison-Kenyon Library
L	Louisiana State Library
LNL-L	Loyola University - Law School, Law Library
LNU	University of New Orleans, Earl K. Long Library
LNX	Xavier University Library
LScS	Southern University & A&M College, Southern University Library
LU	Louisiana State University, Troy H. Middleton Library
LU-L	Louisiana State University, Hebert Law Center Library
MA	Amherst College, Amherst College Library
MB	Boston Public Library
MBMu	Museum of Fine Arts, Boston
MBNU	Northeastern University, Dodge Library
MBSi	Simmons College, Beatley Library
MBU	Boston University, Mugar Memorial Library
MBWI	Wentworth Institute of Technology, Library
MCE/MCW	Episcopal Divnity/Weston School Theology, The Libraries
MCLB	Boston College, Bapst Library
MCM	Massachusetts Institute of Technology, M.I.T. Libraries
MH	Harvard University, Harvard College Library
MH-FA	Harvard University, Fine Arts Library
MH-L	Harvard University, Harvard Law Library
MH-P	Harvard University - Peabody Museum, Tozzer Library
MMeT	Tufts University, Tufts University Library
MMeT-F	Tufts University, Fletcher School, Ginn Library
MNS	Smith College, Library
MSWNEC	Western New England College, Churchill Library
MU	University of Massachusetts/Amherst, University Library

MWA	American Antiquarian Society, Library
MWalB	Brandeis University, Library
MWelC	Wellesley College, Wellesley College Library
May	May Department Stores Company, Corporate Information Center
MdAN	U.S. Naval Academy, Nimitz Library
MdBCS	Coppin State College, Parlett More Library
MdBE	Enoch Pratt Free Library
MdBJ	Johns Hopkins University, Eisenhower Library
MdBLN	Loyola/Notre Dame Library, Inc.
MdBP	Peabody Institute of the Johns Hopkins U, Peabody Conservatory Library
MdU	University of Maryland, College Park, McKeldin Library
MdU-H	University of Maryland, Health Sciences Library
MeU	University of Maine, Fogler Library
MeWC	Colby College, Miller Library
MiBsA	Andrews University, James White Library
MiDU	University of Detroit, Library
MiDW	Wayne State University, Purdy Library
MiDW-M	Wayne State University-Medical School, Shiffman Medical Library
MiEM	Michigan State University, Libraries
MiGrC	Calvin College and Seminary, Library
MiKW	Western Michigan University, Waldo Library
MiMarqN	Northern Michigan University, Olson Library
MiOC	Olivet College, Burrage Library
MiU	University of Michigan - Ann Arbor, University Library
MiYEM	Eastern Michigan University, Eastern Michigan University Library
MnBemS	Bemidji State University, A.C. Clark Library
MnMohC	Concordia College, Carl B. Ylvisaker Library
MnRM	Mayo Clinic, Library
MnS	St. Paul Public Library
MnSC	Concordia College, Buenger Memorial Library
MnSC	St John's University, Alcuin Library
MnSH-L	Hamline University School of Law, Law Library
MnSM	Macalester College, Weyerhaeuser Library
MnSRC	Ramsey County Public Library
MnU	University of Minnesota, Wilson Library
MnU-L	University of Minnesota-Law, Law Library
MoCgS	Southeast Missouri State University, Kent Library
MoKL	Linda Hall Library
MoKU	University of Missouri-Kansas City, Libraries
MoSMa	Maryville College, Library
MoSU	St. Louis University, Pius XII Memorial Library
MoSU-L	St. Louis University, Omar Poos Law Library
MoSW	Washington University in St. Louis, University Libraries
MoSpD	Drury College, Walker Library
MoSpE	Evangel College, Evangel College Library
MoStcL	Lindenwood Colleges, M.L. Butler Library
MoU	University of Missouri-Columbia, Ellis Library
MoWarbT	Central Missouri State University, Ward Edwards Library
MoWgT/W	Eden-Webster Libraries
MsHaU	University of Southern Mississippi, Cook Library
MsJMCL	Mississippi College - School of Law, Law Library
MsLC	Mississippi Library Commission

MsU	University of Mississippi, John Davis Williams Library
MsU-L	University of Mississippi, Law School Library
MtBC	Montana State University, Renne Library
MtDiW	Western Montana College, Lucy Carson Memorial Library
MtHaN	Northern Montana College, Library
MtU	University of Montana, Mansfield Library
N	New York State Library
NAlU	SUNY at Albany, University Libraries
NBPol	Polytechnic Institute of New York, Library
NBiSU	SUNY at Binghamton, Glenn G. Bartle Library
NBrockU	SUNY College at Brockport, Drake Memorial Library
NBuC	State University College at Buffalo, E. H. Butler Library
NBuU	SUNY at Buffalo, Library
NBuU-L	SUNY at Buffalo - Law Library
NCH	Hamilton College, Burke Library
NCaS	St. Lawrence University, Owen D. Young Library
NCortU	SUNY College at Cortland, Memorial Library
NFQ	Queens College, Queens College Library
NFredU	State University College, Reed Library
NHemH	Hofstra University, Hofstra University Library
NIC	Cornell University, Cornell University Libraries
NIlH	Herkimer County Community College, Library
NN	New York Public Library, Research Libraries
NNC	Columbia University, Butler Library
NNC-T	Columbia University, Teachers College Library
NNF	Fordham University, Fordham University Library
NNL	Herbert H. Lehman College, Library
NNLS	New York Law School Library
NNMan	Manhattan College, Cardinal Hayes Library
NNU	New York University, Bobst Library
NOneoU	SUNY College at Oneonta, J.M. Milne Library
NOsU	State University College at Oswego, Penfield Library
NOwU	SUNY College at Old Westbury, Library
NPotU	SUNY at Potsdam, F.W.Crumb Memorial Library
NPurU	SUNY College at Purchase, Library
NRNC	Nazareth College Of Rochester, Lorette Wilmot Library
NRRI	Rochester Institute of Technology, Wallace Memorial Library
NRU	University of Rochester, Library
NSbIA	Institute for Advan.Stud.of Wld.Religion, Library
NSbSU	SUNY at Stony Brook, Melville Library
NSchU	Union College, Schaffer Library
NSySC	Supreme Court at Syracuse, Library
NSyU	Syracuse University, Syracuse University Libraries
NUtSU	SUNY College of Technology at Utica/Rome, Library
NValhW	Westchester Community College, Learning Resource Center
NWM	U.S. Military Academy, Library
Nb-LC	Nebraska Library Commission
NbFrM	Midland Lutheran College, Luther Library
NbKS	Kearney State College, Calvin T. Ryan Library
NbOC	Creighton University, Alumni Memorial Library
NbOMC	Metropolitan Technical Community College, Library
NbSeT	Concordia Teachers College, Lind Library

NbU	University of Nebraska-Lincoln, Libraries
NcAU	University of North Carolina-Asheville, Ramsey Library
NcBoA	Appalachian State University, Belk Library
NcC	Public Library of Charlotte/Mecklenburg,
NcCU	University of North Carolina-Charlotte, J. Murrey Atkins Library
NcCuW	Western Carolina University, Hunter Library
NcD	Duke University, William R. Perkins Library
NcD-L	Duke University, Duke Univ. School of Law Library
NcDaD	Davidson College, Davidson College Library
NcDurCLS	North Carolina Central University, School of Library Science
NcGU	Univ. of North Carolina at Greensboro, Jackson Library
NcGrE	East Carolina University, Joyner Library
NcRS	North Carolina State University, D. H. Hill Library
NcU	University of North Carolina, Wilson Library
NcU-H	University of North Carolina-Chapel Hill, Health Sciences Library, 223 H
NcWfSB	Southeastern Baptist Theo. Seminary
NcWsW	Wake Forest University, Z. Smith Reynolds Library
NdFA	North Dakota State University, The Library
NdU	University of North Dakota, Chester Fritz Library
NhD	Dartmouth College, Dartmouth College Library
NhMSA	St. Anselm College, Geisel Library
NhPlS	Plymouth State College, Lamson Library
NhU	University of New Hampshire, Dimond Library
NjP	Princeton University, Princeton University Library
NjPT	Princeton Theological Seminary, Speer Library
NjParB	Bergen Comm. College
NjR	Rutgers University, Alexander Library
NjTS	Trenton State College, West Library
NjWP	William Paterson College of New Jersey, Sarah Burd Askew Library
NmHo	Hobbs Public Library
NmPE	Easern New Mexico University, Golden Library
NmScW	Western New Mexico University, Miller Library
NmSoI	New Mexico Tech., Martin Speare Memorial Library
NmU	University of New Mexico, General Library
O	Ohio State Library, State Library of Ohio
OAU	Ohio University, Ohio University Library
OAdN	Ohio Northern University, Heterick Memorial Library
OAkU	University of Akron, Beirce Library
OCEPA	U.S. Environmental Protection Agency, Library
OCH	Hebrew Union Coll.-Jewish Inst. of Rel., Klau Library
OCU	University of Cincinnati, Central Library
OCX	Xavier University, MacDonald Library
OClU-L	Cleveland State University, Cleveland-Marshall Coll.Law Library
OClW	Case Western Reserve Univ. Libraries
ODaU	University of Dayton, Roesch Library
ODaWU	Wright State University, University Library
OKentC	Kent State Universty, Kent State University Libraries
OLanU	Ohio University - Lancaster, Library
OLor	Lorain Public Library
OMans	Mansfield-Richland County Public Library,
OOxM	Miami University, Edgar W. King Library
OSW	Wittenberg University, Thomas Library

OTU-L	University of Toledo College of Law, College of Law Library
OU	Ohio State University, Main Library
OU-ED	Ohio State University, Edgar Dale Media Center
OUa	Upper Arlington Public Library
OWest	Porter Public Library
OWoC	College of Wooster, Andrews Library
OYU	Youngstown State University, Maag Library
OkBetC	Bethany Nazarene College, R.T. Williams Learning Resources Ctr
OkOkU-L	Oklahoma City University, Law Library
OkS	Oklahoma State University, Library
OkTOR	Oral Roberts University, Oral Roberts University Library
OkTU	University of Tulsa, McFarlin Library
OkU	University of Oklahoma, University of Oklahoma Libraries
OkU-L	University of Oklahoma Law Center, O.U. Law Center Library
OrCS	Oregon State University, Oregon State University Library
OrStbM	Mount Angel Abbey, Mount Angel Abbey Library
OrU	University of Oregon, Library
PAtM	Muhlenberg College, Muhlenberg-Cedar Crest Libraries
PBBS	Bloomsburg State College, Andruss Library
PBL	Lehigh University, Lehigh University Libraries
PCalS	California State College, Louis L. Manderino Library
PCarlA	U.S. Army War College, U.S. Army War College Library
PHi	Historical Society of Pennsylvania
PKuS	Kutztown State College, Rohrbach Library
PLatS	St. Vincent College, St. Vincent College Library
PLhS	Loch Haven State College, Stevenson Library
PLibCon	Conoco Inc. - Coal Research Division
PNc	New Castle Public Library
PPAmP	American Philosophical Society Library,
PPL	Library Company of Philadelphia
PPPTe	Philadelphia College of Textiles & Sci, Pastore Library
PPSJ	Saint Joseph's University, Drexel Library
PPT	Temple University, Samuel Paley Library
PPiAC	Community College of Allegheny County, CCAC Allegheny Campus Library
PPiCC	Chatham College, Jennie King Mellon Library
PPiD	Duquesne University, Duquesne University Library
PPiPP	Point Park College, Helen Sean Moore Library
PPiU	University of Pittsburgh, Hillman Library
PRosC	Rosemont College, Gertrude Kistler Memorial Library
PSC	Swarthwore College, McCabe Library
PSC-Hi	Swarthmore College, Friends Historical Library
PScU	University of Scranton, Alumni Memorial Library
PSelS	Susquehanna University, Roger M. Blough Learning Center
PShS	Shippensburg State College, Ezra Lehman Memorial Library
PSt	Pennsylvania State University, Pattee Library
PSt-Ca	Pennsylvania State Univ. Capitol Campus, Heindel Library
PU	University of Pennsylvania, Van Pelt Library CH
PWbW	Wilkes College, Eugene Shedden Farley Library
PWcT	West Chester State College, Francis Harvey Green Library
PWmL	Lycoming College
RBrRW	Roger Williams College, Library
RHi	Rhode Island Historical Society, Library

RPPC	Providence College, Phillips Memorial Library
RU	University of Rhode Island, University Library
SLSC	Southern California Rapid Transit Dist.
ScGF	Furman University, James Buchannan Duke Library
ScRhW	Winthrop College, Winthrop College Library
ScU	University of South Carolina, Thomas Cooper Library
ScU-L	University of South Carolina, Law Library
Sd	South Dakota State Library
SdAbN	Northern State College, Williams Library
SdB	South Dakota State University, Hilton M. Briggs Library
SdRM	South Dakota Sch. of Mines & Technology, Devereaux Library
SdSifC	Sioux Falls College, Norman B. Mears Library
SoCleU	Clemson University, Cooper Library
TC	Chattanooga Hamilton Cnty. Bicen.Library,
TCNC	Carson-Newman College, Carson-Newman College Library
TCleL	Lee College, Lee Memorial Library
TKL	Knoxville-Knox County Public Library, Lawson McGhee Library
TMM	Memphis State University, University Libraries
TMaU	University of Tennessee at Martin, Paul Meek Library
TNJ	Vanderbilt University, Vanderbilt University Library
TU	University of Tennessee, James D. Hoskins Library
TxArU	University of Texas at Arlington, UTA Library
TxBeaL	Lamar University, Mary & John Gray Library
TxBelM	University of Mary Hardin-Baylor, Townsend Memorial Library
TxCM	Texas A & M University, Sterling C. Evans Library
TxCaW	West Texas State University, Cornette Library
TxClcU	University of Houston - Clear Lake City, Library and Learning Resources
TxComS	East Texas State University, James Gee Library
TxDN	North Texas State University, University Libraries
TxDW	Texas Woman's University, Texas Woman's University Library
TxDaM	Southern Methodist University, Central University Libraries
TxDaM-P	Southern Methodist University, Bridwell Library-Perkins School
TxDaU	University of Dallas, Main Library
TxEU	University of Texas at El Paso, Library - Serials
TxEdP	Pan American University, Learning Resource Center
TxFTC	Texas Christian University, Mary Couts Burnett Library
TxGML	Texas A&M University at Galveston
TxH	Houston Public Library
TxHR	Rice University, Fondren Library
TxLT	Texas Tech University, Texas Tech University Library
TxLT-L	Texas Tech University - Law School, School of Law Library
TxLarU	Laredo State University, Harold R. Yeary Library
TxSaC	San Antonio College, Library
TxSaT	Trinity University, Library
TxSaU	University of Texas at San Antonio, Library
TxU	University of Texas at Austin, General Libraries
TxU-Da	University of Texas at Dallas, McDermott Library
UCS	Southern Utah State College
UOW	Weber State College, Steward Library
UPB	Brigham Young University, Harold B. Lee Library
UU	University of Utah, University Libraries
ViBlbV	Virginia Polytechnic Inst & State Univ, Libraries

Appendix B - List of NUC Symbols

ViBrC	Bridgewater College, Alexander Mack Memorial Library
ViEmoE	Emory & Henry College, Frederick T. Kelly Library
ViFGM	George Mason University, Fenurick Library
ViHart	James Madison University, Madison Memorial Library
ViPetS	Virginia State University, Johnston Memorial Library
ViU	University of Virginia, Alderman Library
ViU-L	University of Virginia-Law, Law Library
ViW	College of William and Mary, Swem Library
ViW-L	College of Wiliam and Mary-Law, Marshall-Wythe Law Library
ViWisC	Clinch Valley College, John Cook Wyllie Library
VtMiM	Middlebury College, Starr Library
VtU	University of Vermont, Bailey/Howe Library
WAL	Lawrence University, Seeley G. Mudd Library
WEU	University of Wisconsin - Eau Claire, McIntyre Library
WGrU	University of Wisconsin-Green Bay, Library Learning Center
WHi	State Historical Society of Wisconsin, Library
WKenU	University of Wisconsin-Parkside, Library/Learning Center
WLacU	University of Wisconsin - La Crosse, Murphy Library
WMMCW	Medical College of Wisconsin, Todd Wehr Library
WMUW	University of Wisconsin-Milwaukee, Golda Meir Library
WMenU	University of Wisconsin-Stout, Library Learning Center
WRFC	University of Wisconsin - River Falls, Chalmer Davee Library
WSpU	University of Wisconsin-Stevens Point, Learning Resources Center
WU	University of Wisconsin-Madison, Memorial Library
WU-L	University of Wisconsin- Madison, Law Library
WU-M	University of Wisconsin-- Madison, Middleton Health Sciences Library
WWhiwU	University of Wisconsin-Whitewater, Harold Andersen Library
WaChenE	Eastern Washington University, JFK Library
WaOE	Evergreen State College, Daniel J. Evans Library 2300
WaPTP	Pacific Lutheran University, Mortvedt Library
WaPS	Washington State University, Holland Library
WaSpG	Gonzaga University, Crosby Library
WaSpG-L	Gonzaga University, Law School Library
WaSpW	Whitworth College Library
WaTU-L	University of Puget Sound, Univ. of Puget Sound-Law Library
WaU	University of Washington, University of Washington Libraries
WaVC	Clark College, Clark College Library
WvGlS	Glenville State College
WvICG	West Virginia College of Graduate Study, Library
WvU	West Virginia University, West Virginia University Library
WyU	University of Wyoming, University of Wyoming Library

Appendix C

Libraries That did not Return Any of the
Survey Response Forms and Sent No Other Reply

Key: ARL - Member of the Association of Research Libraries
      ACRL - Library represented in ACRL University Library Statistics
           (This is a group of 103 libraries, next-largest after ARL)
      CARL - Member of the Canadian Association of Research Libraries
      IRLA - Member of the Independent Research Libraries Association

----

Library	Affiliation
Adelphi University Library	ACRL
Auburn University at Montgomery	ACRL
Ball State University Library	ACRL
Baylor University Library	ACRL
Bowling Green State Univ. Library	ACRL
CUNY - Library of the Grad. School	ACRL
Carnegie-Mellon University Library	ACRL
Clark University Library	ACRL
Georgetown University Library	ARL
Illinois Inst. of Technology Lib.	ACRL
Loyola Univ. of Chicago Libraries	ACRL
Mississippi State Univ. Library	ACRL
New Mexico State Univ. Library	ACRL
New School for Social Res. Library	ACRL
New York Academy of Medicine Lib.	IRLA
New York Historical Society Library	IRLA
Newberry Library	ARL/IRLA
Purdue University Library	ARL
Rockefeller Univ. Library	ACRL
U.S. International Univ. Library	ACRL
Universite du Quebec a Montreal	CARL
University of California - LA	ARL
University of Chicago Library	ARL
University of Delaware Library	ARL
University of Florida Libraries	ARL
University of Missouri - Rolla	ACRL
University of Nevada - Reno	ACRL
University of Regina	CARL
University of Toledo Library	ACRL
Utah State University Library	ACRL
Virginia Commonwealth U. Library	ACRL
Yeshiva University Libraries	ACRL

Appendix D

Microform Sets Covered in the Clearinghouse Data Base

This list includes all sets listed by libraries in response to Part II of the Microform Project Survey. Although the main focus of the Microform Project is upon collections of books and serials, some publishers supplied the names other types of microform collections as well, and, as a courtesy, these were added to the list of sets that accompanied the survey questionnaire.

In response to the survey, libraries contributed data on these and other microform collections containing materials other than books and serials as well. Since it would otherwise be lost, this information was added to the data base, and for this reason, this list includes entries for a number of series titles as well as oral history, dissertation, and manuscript collections.

The list is in alphabetical order. Upper-case words (such as the initialism ERIC) appear before words in upper- and lower-case letters. The form of title used is derived from three sources: research done by Suzanne Cates Dodson for the second edition of her book, <u>Microform Research Collections: A Guide</u> (1983, Meckler Publishing, Westport, CT); 2) additions and corrections made by microform publishers; and 3) further additions provided by responding libraries.

Unfortunately, sets are often referred to by numerous conventional and short-hand titles. Some sets are cited one way by their publishers and other ways by holding libraries. As Mrs. Dodson points out in the first edition of the <u>Guide</u>, establishing a formal title for a set can be difficult work. Libraries frequently use titles that vary from the forms preferred by publishers. Publishers sometimes change titles for any of a number of marketing purposes, and some publishers include the same works in two or more different sets. These and other idiosyncrasies of microform publishing and of identification of microforms in libraries make the task of establishing formal titles nearly impossible. Mrs. Dodson attempts to alleviate the problem by providing a wealth of information on each set covered in the <u>Guide</u> and by indexing each of them as well.

As an aid to identifying entries, this list contains the name of a publisher, in abbreviated form. The publisher cited is not necessarily the original nor the current supplier of the set. It is simply the organization specified in the source used for the title (the Dodson <u>Guide</u>, the publisher itself, or a holding library). In a few cases where more than one publisher is known, more than one publisher is given. The abbreviations are not intended to be cryptic. Nonetheless, a brief cross-reference list is given at the close of the list.

Appendix D - Sets in the Clearinghouse Data Base

The four-digit number that follows publisher abbreviations is the code used in identifying the set in the Clearinghouse data base. A number of cross-references appear in the list. These cite entries by number rather than titles. Insofar as possible, sets were numbered in alphabetical order. Certain exceptions had to be made where more sets were reported in a given alphabetic location than there were numbers available to identify. In other cases the title of a set was changed after numbering (e.g. ERIC, which was first alphabetized under "United States" and therefore bears the number 3490). Thus in most cases, though not all, the numbers can be used to find sets in the list. A list of sets in numeric order is available from the Project office on request.

A.S.W. Rosenbach. Early American Children's Books (See 2890)
ABA Section Proceedings (Atlas Microfilming) 0004
ACIR, Collected Publications of the U.S. Advisory Commission on
   Intergovernmental Relations on Microfiche (PDF) 0005
ACRL Microcard Series (See 0010)
ACRL Microform Series (Microcard) 0010
AFL-CIO Pamphlets, 1889-1955 (Greenwood) 0012
ALF, Archives de la Linguistique Francaise (See 0420)
AM-I Collection of Sheet Music to 1830 (Brookhaven) 0017
APS, American Periodicals Series (See 0261-0263)
ASI Microfiche Library (American Statistics Index/Microfiche Library) (CIS) 0500
Academia de la Historia, Madrid. Memorial Historico Espanol: Coleccion de
   Documentos ... que Publica la Real Academia (Microcard) 0008
Academie des Sciences, Paris. Comptes rendus hebdomodaires (Microcard) 0009
Adelaide Nutting History Nursing Collection from the History of Nursing Collection,
   Teachers College, Columbia University (UMI) 0018
Administrative Histories of U.S. Civilian Agencies: Korean War (RP) 0020
Administrative Histories of U.S. Civilian Agencies: World War II (RP) 0030
Africa. Special Studies (Univ Pub Am) 0035
African Documents (General/Erasmus) 0040
African Library (Hachette) 0050
African Official Statistical Serials (Chadwyck-Healey) 0060
African Official Statistics (IDC) 0070
Afro-American History Series (SRI) 0073
Afro-American Rare Book Collection (Kistler) 0075
Afro-American Studies Materials (Lost Cause) 0080
Agardh, Jacob Georg. species, Genera et Ordines Algarum (Microcard) 0085
Agrarian Periodicals in the United States 1920-1960 (Greenwood/CIS) 0090
Agricultural Publications (B & H) 0100
Agricultural Publications (Spaulding Co) 0101
Almanach National (Microcard) 0105
America 1935-1946 (Chadwyck-Healey) 0110
American Anti-Slavery Pamphlets (See 0380)
American Antiquarian Society, Worcester, Mass. Early American Newspapers (See 1250)
American Architectural Books (RP) 0120
American Archives (Johnson Reprint) 0113
American Autobiographies: Series I (Brookhaven) 0131
American Autobiographies: Series II (Brookhaven) 0132
American Autobiographies: Series III (Brookhaven) 0133
American Autobiographies: Series IV (Brookhaven) 0134

American Autobiographies: Series V (Brookhaven) 0135
American Bibliography. Evans and Shaw-Shoemaker (See 1231/1232)
American Children's Books. A.S.W. Rosenbach Collection (See 2890)
American Church Records. Series I-III (Ecum Res Agency) 0138
American City Directories (See 0990)
American Civil Liberties Union Records and Publications (MCA) 0015
American Colonial Records (See 2700)
American Culture Series (See also 1220)
American Culture: Series I, 1493-1806 (UMI) 0141
American Culture: Series II, 1493-1875 (UMI) 0142
American Directories Through 1860 (See 0990)
American Federation of Labor (See 0012)
American Fiction 1774-1900 (RP) 0151
American Fiction 1774-1900: Lyle H. Wright (Lost Cause) 0160
American Fiction 1901-1910 (RP) 0152
The American Film Institute Seminars: Part I (MCA) 0181
The American Film Institute Seminars: Part II (MCA) 0182
The American Film Institute/Louis B. Mayer Oral History Collection: Part I (MCA) 0171
The American Film Institute/Louis B. Mayer Oral History Collection: Part II (MCA) 0172
American Historical Association. Committee on Documentation. Russian Historical
    Sources (See 2991)
American Imprints Inventory (Microcard) 0187
American Indian Correspondence: The Presbyterian Historical Soc Coll of
    Missionaries Letters (Greenwood) 0190
American Indian Cultural Anthropology (See 3544)
American Indian Periodicals in the Princeton University Library (Clearwater) 0200
American Labor Unions' Constitutions and Proceedings 1836-1974 + supplements (MCA) 0210
American Literary Annuals and Gift Books 1825-1865 (RP) 0220
American Literature and History, Nineteenth Century (See 2490)
American Literature of the 19th Century (See 2490)
American Material in the Liverpool Papers (MicroMethods) 0223
American Natural History (RP) 0230
American Newspapers and Periodicals Published in the U.K. and Europe: 18th-20th
    Centuries (World) 0240
American Newspapers, 1704-1820 (See 1250)
American Periodicals: Series I, 18th Century (UMI) 0261
American Periodicals: Series II, 1800-1850 (UMI) 0262
American Periodicals: Series III, 1850-1900 (UMI) 0263
American Poetry 1609-1900 (RP) 0270
American Prose Fiction [produced by UMI, distributed by RP] (See 0150)
American Psychological Association. Catalog of Selected Documents in Psychology
    (See 2030)
American Revolution. Source Materials Relating to the Struggle for American
    Independence (IHS) 0290
American Slavery Pamphlets (See 3110)
American Society of Papyrologists. Papyrology on Microfiche. Series 1-2 (American
    Society of Papyrologists) 0295
American State Papers (See 0980/3545)
American State Papers 1789-1838 (Brookhaven) 0300
American State Reports Prior to the National Reporter System (Trans Media) 0305
American Statistics Index Microfiche Library (See 0050)
Americana Not in Sabin (General) 0310

Analecta Hymnica Medii Aevi (Microcard) 0317
Ancient Roman Architecture (Clearwater) 0330
Anglia, Zeitschrift fur Englische Philologie (Microcard) 0335
Annual Reports of All Corporations Listed on the American Stock Exchange (Godfrey) 0340
Annual Reports of All Corporations Listed on the New York Stock Exchange (Godfrey) 0350
Annual Reports of Major American Corporations (MIMC) 0358
Annual Reports of the Major American Companies (MIMC) 0360
Anti-Slavery Collection: 18th-19th Centuries from the Library of the Society of
    Friends (World) 0370
Anti-Slavery Propaganda in the Oberlin College Library (Lost Cause) 0380
Arbitration in the Schools (KTO) 0383
Archaeological Survey of Canada. Papers. [Commission archaeologique du Canada.
    Dossier.] (Micromedia) 0381
Architecture of Washington D.C. (Dunlap Society) 0382
Archive Russkoi Revolutsii (Microcard) 0384
Archives Africain (POF/Clearwater) 0390
Archives Canada Microfiches (Pub Arc/Canada) 0410
Archives Diplomatiques (IHS) 0425
Archives Parliamentaires de 1787 a 1868 (Microcard) 0458
Archives and Manuscript Collections in the USSR: Finding Aids on Microfiche (IDC) 0400
Archives de la Linguistique Francaise: Coll de Documents Relatifs a la Langue
    Francaise 1500-1900 (France-Expansion) 0420
Archives of American Publishers (Chadwyck-Healey) 0430
Archives of Archaeology (U of Wisconsin Press) 0436
Archives of British Men of Science (Mansell) 0438
The Archives of British Publishers on Microfilm (Chadwyck-Healey) 0440
Archives of British Trade Unions (Harvester) 0450
Archives of Plaid Cymru 1926-81 and continuation (World) 0455
Archives of Psychology (Johnson Associates) 0385
Archives of Psychology (NCR) 0456
Archives of the Communist Party of Great Britain (World) 0452
El Archivo de Hidalgo de Parral 1631-1821 (B & H) 0460
Archivo de Musica Sacra (Catedra Metro Mexico) 0465
Art Exhibition Catalogues on Microfiche (Chadwyck-Healey) 0470
Art History Project: Rare Works on Microfiche (IDC) 0480
Art Periodicals on Microform (Chadwyck-Healey) 0490
Asian Statistics (IDC) 0510
Association of College and Research Libraries. ACRL Microform Series (See 0010)
Atlanta University. Library. Black Culture Collection (See 0540)
Attorney General Reports and Opinions (Trans Media) 0527
Attorneys General Opinions, by State (Hein) 0525
B.F. Stevens's Facsimiles of Manuscripts in European Archives Relating to America,
    1773-1783 (AMS) 0528
Baedeker's Handbook for Travellers (Greenwood) 0529
Bartlett, John Russell. The Mexican Boundary Commission Papers of J.R. Bartlett
    (See 2321)
Bell and Howell's Black Culture Collection (See 0540)
Bell's British Theatre Collection (Microcard) 0530
Berger Commission (See 2280)
Bergquist, G. William. Three Centuries of English and American Plays (See 3320)
Bexar Archives of Texas (Univ Texas at Austin) 0533
Bibliotheca Americana (See 3060)

Appendix D - Sets in the Clearinghouse Data Base

Bibliotheque Africaine (See 0050)
Bibliotheque Linguistique Americaine (Microcard) 0535
Biofiche (Biosciences Inf Serv) 0537
Black Culture Collection (B & H) 0540
Black Journals: Phase I (Greenwood/CIS) 0543
Black Journals: Phase II (Greenwood/CIS) 0544
Black Studies: Schomburg Center for Research in Black Culture (See 3040/3042)
Blodgett Collection of Spanish Civil War Pamphlets (Harvard College Lib) 0546
Book Catalogs of American Law Libraries (Brookhaven) 0547
Books About North American Indians on Microfilm (MCA) 0560
Books Printed in the Low Countries before 1601 (General) 0580
Books Printed in the Netherlands and Belgium Before 1601 (See 0580)
Books and Pamphlets on East Africa (Kenya Archives) 0565
Books for College Libraries (IHS) 0570
Botany Library on Microfiche (IDC) 0590
Britain and Europe since 1945 (Harvester) 0600
British Architectural Library. Drawings Collection (World) 0630
British Architectural Library. Microfilmed Collection of Rare Books (World) 0640
British Architectural Library. Unpublished Manuscripts (World) 0650
British Birth Control Material at the British Library of Political and Economic
    Sciences 1800-1947 (World) 0660
British Culture: Series I, 18th and 19th Century (Lost Cause) 0671
British Culture: Series II (Lost Cause) 0672
British Culture: Series III and onward (Lost Cause) 0673
British Government Non-Parliamentary Publications on Microform (Chadwyck-Healey) 0690
British Government Publications Containing Statistics 1801-1977 on Microfilm
    (Chadwyck-Healey) 0700
British Industry, Labour and Trade Unionism 1887-1934 (Harvester) 0710
British Labour History Ephemera 1880-1900 and 1900-1926 (World) 0720
British Law Reports (Trans Media) 0725
British Manuscripts Project (UMI) 0728
British Nineteenth Century Freethought Books (World) 0727
British Official Publications Not Published by HMSO (Chadwyck-Healey) 0730
British Periodicals in the Creative Arts (UMI) 0740
British Periodicals of the 18th and 19th Centuries (See 1270)
British Periodicals, Literary Series (See 1440)
British Political Sources Series (Harvester) 0742
British Publishers' Archives on Microfilm (Chadwyck-Healey) 0744
British Records relating to America in Microform (EP) 0750
British Trade Union History Collection (World) 0770
British and Continental Rhetoric and Elocution (UMI) 0610
British and European Publishers' Catalogs Annual (Chadwyck-H/MRI) 0620
British and Foreign State Papers (MIMC) 0625
British and Foreign State Papers (Microcard/LC) 0626
Bureau of Indian Affairs Annual Reports (Microcard) 0775
A Business History Collection on Microfiche (RP) 0780
CBS News Review (See 0781)
CBS News on Microfiche (MCA) 0930
CIA Collection (UPDATA) 0965
CIO, Congress of Industrial Organizations (See 0012)
CIS Microfiche Library (CIS) 0970
CIS Periodicals on Microfiche (CIS) 0975

CIS U.S. Serial Set on Microfiche (CIS) 0980
Calendar of Virginia State Papers (Microcard) 0783
California County and Regional Histories (See 1096)
Cambridge Texts in the History of Chinese Medicine (Cambridge Univ Press) 0785
Camden Society. London. Publications (Microcard/AMS) 0786
Camden Society. London. Publications. New Series (Microcard/AMS) 0787
Can - Fil (B & H) 0790
Canada Labour Papers on Microfilm in the Labour Canada Library (Pub Arc/Canada) 0815
Canada. Archives. Pamphlets in the Public Archives of Canada (Pub Arc/Canada) 0800
Canada. National Gallery. Exhibition Catalogues, 1919-1959 (See 1465)
Canada. National Library. Peel Bibliography (See 2560)
Canada. Ontario Ministry of Education. Research Reports (See 2847)
Canada. Parliament. Unprinted Sessional Papers. 1916- (Micromedia) 0810
Canadian Art Microdocuments/Microdocuments d'Art Canadien (Nat Gal Canada) 0820
Canadian Association in Support of the Native Peoples: Vertical Files (Micromedia) 0830
Canadian Curriculum Guides (Micromedia) 0840
Canadian Historical Documents. Lawrence Lande Collection (See 2113)
Canadian Imprints 1751-1800 (Pub Arc/Can) 0850
Canadian Institute for Historical Micro-Reproduction: Microfiche Collection (CIHM) 0860
Canadian Labour Papers on Microfilm (Pub Arc/Canada) 0865
Canadian Music Centre, Toronto. Microfilm Project (Publisher Unknown) 0864
Canadian Newspapers on Microfilm (CLA) 0870
Canadian Parliamentary Proceedings and Sessional Papers 1841-1970 (HDI) 0880
Canadian Royal Commissions (See 1480)
Canadian Studies Program (Micro Ctr/Texas) 0890
Canadian Studies Series. Univ of Rochester Press (See 3551)
Canadian Theses on Microfiche (Nat Lib Canada) 0893
Canadian Theses on Microfilm (Pub Arc/Canada) 0894
Canadian Urban Sources (See 3570)
Canadian Whites: Wartime Comics on Microfiche (B & H) 0900
Canadiana (Staton and Boyle) (IHS) 0910
Canadiana 1751-1800 (See 0850)
Canadiana in the Toronto Public Library (See 0910)
Canadiana on Microfiche (Nat Lib Canada) 0918
Canadiana on Microfilm (General) 0920
Canedex: Canadian Education Monographs on Microfiche (Micromedia) 0930
Catalog of Selected Documents in Psychology (See 2030)
Censorship in Tsarist Russia (See 2910)
Ch'en, Ch'eng. Collection (Hoover Institution) 0934
Charles Sanders Pierce: Complete Published Works, Including Selected Materials
    (Johnson Associates) 0931
Chaucer Society, London. Publications. Series 1-2 (Microcard) 0932
Chiao T'ung Shih (Ctr Chinese Res Mat) 0933
Chicago Visual Library. Text-Fiche Publications (U of Chicago Pr) 0935
Chicano Studies Library Serial Collection (Lib Microfilms) 0940
Child Behavior and Comparative Psychology (See 1619)
China Coast Newspapers (Ctr Res Libs) 0941
Chinese Maritime Customs Publications (Harvard Univ Lib Mic) 0942
Chinese Oral History Collection (MCA) 0943
Chinese and Japanese Buddhist Materials in Microform (Inst Adv St Wld Rel) 0944
The Christ Church, Oxford, Collection (Harvester) 0945
Christie's Pictorial Archive (Mindata) 0950

Church Missionary Society. Proceedings on the Society for Missions to Africal and
    the East, 1801-1921 (Micro Methods) 0955
Church Missionary Society. West Indies Mission Records, 1819-1861 (Micro Methods) 0956
Church, State and Politics in Sixteenth- and Seventeenth-Century England (Harvester) 0960
City Directories of the United States (RP) 0990
Civil War 1861-1865 (MCA) 0995
Clark, T.D. Travels in the New South (See 3390/3391)
Clark, T.D. Travels in the Old South (See 3400/3402/3403)
Classics of International Law (Trans Media) 0996
Code of Federal Regulations (Oceana) 0994
Coleccion de Documentos Ineditos: 1) Para la Historia de Espana, 2) Relativos al
    Descubrimiento ... America y Oceania (Microcard) 0997
Coleccion de Libros Cubanos (KTO) 0998
Collected Papers of Charles Wilson Peale and His Family (Kraus) 1002
Collection Adrien Arcand (Ctr Rech Hist) 0998
Collection de Documents Relatifs a l'Histoire de Paris Pendant la Revolution
    Francaise... (Brookhaven) 0999
Collection of Newspapers Relating to Centennial Celebrations and Histories of
    United States Localities (Publisher Unknown) 1003
College Catalog Collection, Microfiche (Nat Micro Lib) 1000
College Catalog Library (Career Guidance Fn) 1001
College Catalogs on Microfiche - Micrologue (Am Micro-Data) 1010
Colonial Records of the American Colonies (See 2700)
Columbia University Oral History Collection (MCA) 1020
Columbia University. Teachers College. Contributions to Education (AMS) 1022
Comptes Rendus Hebdomodaires... (See 0009)
Concordances and Texts of the Royal Scriptorum Manuscripts of Alfonso X el Sabio
    (Hispan Sem/Med Stud) 1043
La Condition Ouvriere en France au 19e Siecle (Hachette) 1025
Conditions and Politics in Occupied Western Europe 1940-1945 (Harvester) 1030
Cone Tanjur (Lib of Congress) 1035
Confederate Imprints (RP) 1040
Confederate State Dept Records ("Pickett Papers") (See 2811)
Congress of Industrial Organizations (See 0012)
Conspiracy Trials in America, 1918-1953 (Michael Glazier) 1045
Constitutions and Laws of the American Indian (Publisher Unknown) 1047
Contemporary Legal Periodical Series (Rothman) 1055
Contemporary Newspapers of the North American Indian (B & H) 1060
Contributions to Education (See 1022)
The Controller's Library Collection of Her Majesty's Stationery Office Publications
    1922-1977 (HDI) 1070
Cornell Petrarch Collection (Kraus) 1083
The Cornell University Collection of Women's Rights Pamphlets (B & H) 1080
Corporate Microfile (National Databank) 1085
Corporation Annual Reports [Godfrey] (See 3040/3050)
Corporation Files (IHS) 1090
Corpus Scriptorum Ecclesiasticorum Latinorum (Microcard) 1094
Corpus Scriptorum Historiae Byzantiae (Microcard) 1093
County Histories of the Old Northwest (RP) 1095
County and Regional Histories (RP) 1096
Covent Garden Prompt Books (B & H) 1097
The Cox Library (Americana Unlim) 1110

Crandall, M.J. Confederate Imprints (See 1040)
Crime and Juvenile Delinquency (MCA) 1120
Crime, Criminology and Civil Liberties (Harvester) 1130
Current National Statistical Compendiums on Microfiche (CIS/Greenwood) 1140
Curriculum Development Library (Fearon Pitman) 1150
Curriculum Guides in Microfiche 1970-1980 (Kraus) 1160
Curriculum Materials Microfile (UMI) 1163
DRUGDEX, 1977- (Micromedex) 1204
Daniel Defoe Pamphlet Collection (See 3855)
De Bonneville, Nicolas (See 2478)
Declassified Documents Reference System 1975- (Carrollton) 1170
Declassified Documents Reference System Retrospective Collection (Carrollton/RP) 1171
Decouvertes et Establissements des Francais dans l'Ouest et dans le Sud de
     l'Amerique Septentionale, 1878-1888 (See 2401)
Defoe, Daniel. Pamphlet Collection (See 3855)
Defoe, Daniel. Writings (See 3855)
Denkmaler Deutscher Tonkunst (Univ Music Editions) 1173
Dibden's Theater (Microcard) 1175
Dibden, Thomas John. The London Theatre (See 1175)
Diccionario Enciclopedico Hispano-Americano de la Literatura, Ciencias y Artes, v.
     1-28 (Montaner y Simon) 1178
Dime Novels (UMI) 1180
Dime Novels Collection (Lib of Congress) 1181
Disclosure (Disclosure) 1190
Dissertation Abstracts (UMI) 1185
Documentos Ineditos (See 0997)
Documents Relatifs a l'Histoire de Paris (See 0999)
Documents of the National Security Council (Univ Pub Am) 1195
Documents on Contemporary China 1949-1975 (Kraus/Johnson) 1200
Dodsley, Robert. A Select Collection of Old English Plays (Microcard) 1198
Douglass Collection of Religious Research Projects (See 3160)
Douglass, H. P. Social Problems and the Churches (See 3160)
Draper Manuscripts From the Wisconsin Historical Society (MCA/U of Chic/SHSW) 1203
Dugdale-Monasticon Anglicanum (Microcard) 1205
Duke Indian Oral History Collection (Kraus/Johnson) 1210
ELPS, Early English Periodicals (See 1440)
ERIC. Educational Resources Information Center Reports (ERIC) 3490
ESTC (Eighteenth Century Short Title Catalog) (See 1328)
Early American Books and Pamphlets in the Field of Art and Architecture (from the
     American Culture Series) (UMI) 1220
Early American Children's Books. Rosenbach Collection (See 2890)
Early American Imprints: First Series (Evans) 1639-1800 (Readex) 1231
Early American Imprints: Second Series (Shaw-Shoemaker) 1801-1819 (Readex) 1232
Early American Medical Imprints (RP) 1240
Early American Newspapers 1704-1820 (Readex) 1250
Early American Orderly Books, 1748-1817 (RP) 1243
Early American Periodicals Index to 1850 (Readex) 1244
Early Architectural Books. Fowler Collection (See 1530)
Early Belgian Books (See 0580)
Early British Fiction: Pre-1750 (RP) 1260
Early British Periodicals (UMI) 1270
Early British Periodicals, Literary (See 1440)

Early Dutch Books (See 0580)
Early English Books: Series I, 1475-1640 (Pollard and Redgrave) (UMI) 1281
Early English Books: Series II, 1641-1700 (Wing) (UMI) 1282
Early English Courtesy Books 1571-1773 (B & H) 1290
Early English Newspapers 1662-1820 + supplements (RP) 1300
Early English Text Society Publications. Original and Extra Series (Microcard) 1303
Early French Books (See 1540)
Early German Books (See 1630)
Early Italian Books (See 1991)
Early Portuguese Books (See 1760)
Early Quaker Writings - Second Series: 17th Century (World) 1316
Early Quaker Writings, 1650-1750 (World) 1315
Early Rare Photographic Books. Series A: The Northwestern Museum of Science and
    Industry Collection (World) 1320
Early Russian Books (See 2690)
Early Spanish Books (See 1760)
Early State Records (See 2813)
Economic and Political Pamphlets, 1700-1870: English (See 1393)
Economics Working Papers (Trans Media) 1323
Ecumenism Research Agency Publications (Ecum Res Agency) 1325
Educational Media Catalogs on Microfiche (Olympic Media Inf) 1327
Educational Resources Information Center (ERIC) (See 1455)
Eighteenth Century Documents. Giroude, France (Publisher Unknown) 1329
Eighteenth Century English Literature (General) 1330
Eighteenth Century French Fiction (See 1570)
Eighteenth Century French Literature (See 1570)
Eighteenth Century Russian Books on Microfilm (See 3010)
The Eighteenth Century: A Microfilm Collection Based on the Eighteenth Century
    Short Title Catalog (ESTC) (RP) 1328
Eighteenth-Century Russian Studies (IDC) 1340
Eighteenth-Century Sources for the Study of English Literature and Culture
    (Micrographics 2) 1350
Emblem Books (IDC) 1355
Energy and Agriculture (MCA) 1355
Energyfiche (EIC) 1360
English Architectural Drawings from the Victoria and Albert Museum (EP) 1380
English Cartoons and Satirical Prints 1320-1832 in the British Museum (Chadwyck-
    Healey) 1390
English Drama (EP) 1392
English Drama, 17th and 18th Centuries (Microcard) 1391
English Economic and Political Pamphlets, 1700-1870 (Publisher Unknown) 1393
The English Gift Books and Literary Annuals 1823-1857 (Chadwyck-Healey) 1400
English Legal Manuscripts Microfiche Project (IDC) 1420
English Linguistics 1500-1800 (Scolar Press) 1430
English Literary Periodicals (UMI) 1440
English Poetry... (Middle English) (Microcard) 1443
The English Reports. Full Reprint (Microcard) 1445
English and American Drama (See 2480)
English and American Plays (See 1370/2480/3320)
English and American Plays of the 19th Century: English Plays 1801-1900; American
    Plays 1831-1900 (Readex) 1370
Envirofiche (EIC) 1450

Espana Sagrada (Microcard) 1456
European Musical Instruments on Prints and Drawings (IDC) 1457
European Official Statistical Serials on Microfiche (Chadwyck-Healey) 1460
Evans, Charles. Early American Imprints (See 1231)
Exhibition Catalogues on Microfiche, 1919-1959. National Gallery of Canada
    (Chadwyck-Healey?) 1465
Explorations Printed in the Documents of the United States Government (See 2840)
FBIS (Foreign Broadcast Information Service) (See 3522)
The Faber Birren Collection of Books on Color (RP) 1470
Facts on Film (Southern Ed Rptg Ser) 1473
Federal Labor and Immigration Reports on Microfiche (Redgrave) 1477
Federal Royal Commissions in Canada 1867-1979 (Micromedia) 1480
Fin-de-Siecle Symbolist and Avant-Garde Periodicals (RP) 1500
Finding Aids on Microfiche (Pub Arc/Canada) 1510
Finnish-Canadian Operetta Manuscript Collection (McLaren Micropub) 1515
Flugschriften des Fruhen 16 Jahrhunderts. Microfiche Serie 1978- (IDC) 1517
Flugschriftensammlung Gustav Frèytag (K. G. Saur) 1518
Focus on English Literature (UMI) 1520
Food and Nutrition (MCA) 1525
Foreign Broadcast Information Service (FBIS) (See 3522)
Four Centuries of Spanish Drama (See 3200)
The Fowler Collection of Early Architectural Books (RP) 1530
France. Giroude. Eighteenth Century Documents (See 1329)
French Books 1601-1700 (General) 1550
French Books before 1601 (General) 1540
French Drama (See 3330)
French Drama Series (See 3330)
French Drama Series, 1957- (Microcard) 1555
French Fiction and Poetry: 18th Century (General) 1570
French Fiction, 18th Century (General) 1560
French Linguistic Archives (See 0420)
French Political Pamphlets (RP) 1580
French Political Pamphlets from 1560 to 1653 (B & H) 1590
French Revolution: Critical Works and Historical Sources (General) 1600
French Revolution: Critical and Historical Literature (See 1600)
French Revolutionary Pamphlets (General) 1610
French Voyagers in the Mediterranean. 16th-18th Centuries (Hachette) 1611
Garma C. C. Chang Collection (Inst Adv St Wld Rel) 1612
Genealogy and Local History, Part 1 (MCA) 1615
Genealogy and Local History, Part 2 (MCA) 1616
Genealogy and Local History, Part 3 (MCA) 1617
Genetic Psychology Monographs; Child Behavior and Comparative Psychology (Johnson
    Associates) 1619
German Baroque Literature: Harold Jantz Collection (RP) 1621
German Baroque Literature: Yale Collection (RP) 1622
German Books before 1601 (General) 1630
German Drama (General) 1640
German Foreign Ministry Archives, 1867-1920 (Univ of Calif) 1642
German Jewish Press on Microfilm (PDF) 1645
German Periodicals and Books from the Wilhelm Scherer Collection (RP) 1650
German Plays in Microform (See 1640)
The Gerritsen Collection of Women's History (MCA) 1660

Gesellschaft fur Musikforschung (Univ Music Editions) 1665
Goldsmiths'-Kress Library of Economic Literature. Segment I: Printed Books Through
    1800 (RP) 1670
Goldsmiths'-Kress Library of Economic Literature. Segment II: 1801-1850 (RP) 1671
Goldsmiths'-Kress Library of Economic Literature. Segment III: Periodicals through
    1850 (RP) 1672
Government Publications Relating to Africa in Microform (See 1675)
Government Publications Relating to African Countries Prior to Independence (EP) 1675
Gray, William S., Research Collection in Reading (See 3750)
Great Black Americans (MCA) 1673
Great Britain. Board of Trade/Overseas Trade Dept. Economic Surveys (See 0690)
Great Britain. Colonial Office. 42 Series (CanArc Microfilms) 1676
Great Britain. Colonial Office. Annual Reports of the Colonies (Andronicus) 1677
Great Britain. Colonial Office. Original Correspondence. Series No. 5 (KTO) 1678
Great Britain. Exchequer and Audit Dept. American Loyalist Claims. Series 1-4,
    1776-1835 (Kraus) 1679
Great Britain. Foreign Office. British and Foreign State Papers (See 0626)
Great Britain. Foreign Office. Records on Mexico (Publisher Unknown) 1680
Great Britain. HMSO (See 1070)
Great Britain. Historical Manuscript Commission. Reports. Series 1-81 (Microcard) 1685
Great Britain. House of Commons. Parliamentary Papers. 1975/76- (Chadwyck-Healey) 1691
Great Britain. House of Lords. Sessional Papers. 1788-1835 (Datamics) 1692
Great Britain. Laws, Statutes. Statutes of the Realm, 1225-1713 (Microcard) 1690
Great Britain. Parliament. Debates (MIMC) 1693
Great Britain. Parliament. Hansard's Parliamentary Debates, Lords and Commons, 1066
    on (Readex) 1694
Great Britain. Parliament. House of Commons (See also 1840)
Great Britain. Parliament. House of Commons, Sessional Papers Indexes, 1696-1900
    (Readex) 1695
Great Britain. Parliament. House of Commons. Sessional Papers. 1731-on (Readex) 1696
Great Britain. Parliament. House of Commons. Sessional Papers. 1731-1800 (Datamics) 1697
Great Britain. Parliament. House of Lords. Sessional Papers 1806-1859 (Trans Media) 1698
Great Britain. Parliament. House of Lords. Sessional Papers. 1940- (Readex) 1699
Great Britain. Parliament. Journal of House of Commons, 1547-1974 (Readex) 1700
Great Britain. Parliament. Journals (MIMC) 1701
Great Britain. Privy Council. Acts of the Privy Council. Colonial Series ... New
    Series (Microcard) 1704
Great Britain. Public Record Office. Rolls Series (See 1703)
Great Britain. Public Record Office. Rerum Britannicarum (See 1703)
Great Britain. War Office. Route Books. Military Reports and Information Precis for
    British Africa, 1867-1912 (EP) 1689
Great Britain. Yearbook. Mayards (Trans Media) 1705
Great Works of American Literature (Readex) 1710
Gregg Music Sources (N.K. Gregg) 1713
HRAF Microfiles (Human Rel Ar F) 1860
Hakluyt Society. Publications. Series 1-2 (Microcard) 1715
Hannah Institute for the History of Medicine Microfiche Project (Hannah Institute) 1714
Harbottle Dorr Collection of Annotated Massachusetts Newspapers, 1765-1777
    (Massachusetts Historical Soc?) 1716
The Harrisburg Newspapers (Publisher Unknown) 1717
Harvard African Studies (AMS) 1718
Harvard Law School Library Microform Project (Harvard Law S L) 1720

Health Care, 1970-1978 + supplements (MCA) 1730
Health, Physical Education and Recreation Microform Publications (U of Oregon) 1740
Hebrew University Oral History Collection (MCA) 1743
Henry Bradshaw Society. Publications (Microcard) 1745
Herbst, Johannes. Collection (See 2024)
Herstory (Women's Hist RC) 1750
Hispanic Culture Series: Spanish, Portuguese and American Books before 1601 (General) 1760
Histoire Litteraire de la France... (Microcard) 1765
Historic American Building Survey (Chadwyck-Healey) 1770
Historic American Building Survey (Lib of Congress) 1771
Historical Data Papers for the Provinces (Nat Lib of Manila) 1773
Historical Legal Periodical Series (Rothman) 1772
History of Chinese Medicine (See 0785)
History of Ideas in Europe (General) 1790
History of Medicine (IDC) 1800
History of Nursing (UMI) 1805
History of Photography (RP) 1810
History of Religion (See 3310)
History of Women (RP) 1830
History of the Office of Censorship (Publisher Unknown) 1818
History of the Pacific Northwest and Canadian Northwest (RP) 1820
Holback and His Friends (Hachette) 1835
The House of Commons Parliamentary Papers 1801-1900 (Chadwyck-Healey) 1840
Housing and Urban Affairs 1965-1976 + supplements (MCA) 1850
Human Environment Microlibrary (Microfiche Publ) 1862
Human Sexuality (See 3080)
IIS Microfiche Library (Index to International Statistics Microfiche Library) (CIS) 1865
IMC-CBMS Archive (International Missionary Council-Conference of British Missionary
    Societies Archive) (IDC) 1861
INFACT Medical School Information System (Dataflow) 1940
Ichthyological Source Materials (Microcard) 1863
Iconographic Index on Dutch and Flemish Painting (Rijksbureau voor Kun) 1864
Immigration Commission Reports, 1907-1910 (Greenwood) 1873
Index Iconologicus (Publisher Unknown) 1888
Index Photographique de l'Art en France (Bild Foto Marb) 1890
Indian Claims Commission Series: The Library of American Indian Affairs (Clearwater) 1900
Indian Pioneer Papers 1860-1935 (Kraus/Johnson) 1910
The Indian Rights Association Papers 1864-1973 (MCA) 1920
Indian Tribal Codes (Univ Washington Law) 1925
Indians of North America (Lost Cause) 1930
Indonesia. "Van Neil" Microfilm Collection (Publisher Unknown) 1933
Ingram, John Henry. Poe Collection in the Univ of Virginia Library (See 2023)
Insider (Micromedia) 1950
The Institute of Chartered Accountants in England and Wales: Microfilmed Coll of
    Rare Books etc (World) 1960
International Population Census Publications (RP) 1970
Irish Newspapers in Dublin Libraries, 1685-1754 (Erasmus) 1975
Irish Political and Radical Newspapers of the 20th Century: Phase I, 1896-1941
    (Irish Micro) 1980
Italian Books 1601-1700 (General) 1992
Italian Books before 1601 (General) 1991
Italian Drama (General) 2000

Italian Drama on Microfilm (See 2000)
JPRS (see 3520/3521)
JSAJ: Catalog of Selected Documents in Psychology (Kraus/Johnson) 2030
Jacob Georg Arardh. Species, Genera et Ordines Algarum (See 0085)
Jacques P. Migne. Patrologie Cursus Completus (See 2375)
Jantz, Harold Stein. German Baroque Literature (See 1621)
Japan. Ministry of Foreign Affairs. Documents, 1868-1945 (Lib of Congress) 2003
Japanese Camp Newspapers, 1942-1945 (Publisher Unknown) 2004
Japanese Monographs (Lib of Congress) 2005
Jazz Periodicals (Greenwood) 2007
Jeffersonian Americana (IHS) 2010
Jesuit Relations and Allied Documents (Microcard) 2015
The Jewish Press in the Netherlands, 1674-1950 [subset of no. 2020] (IDC) 2021
Jewish Studies Microfiche Project (IDC) 2020
Jewish Theological Seminary of America. Incunabula Collection and Steinschneider
    Collection (UMI) 2022
Johannes Herbst Collection (Univ Music Editions) 2024
John Henry Ingram's Poe Collection (Univ of Virginia Lib) 2023
Joint Publications Research Service (See 3520/3521)
Journaux Ephemeres de la Periode de la Revolution (See 3066)
Journaux Ephemeres, 1848-1850 (See 3065)
Journaux Ephemeres, 1869-1871 (See 3064)
Journaux, Periode de la Commune (ACRPP) 2025
Kellog Child Art Collection (See 2850)
Kentucky 1000 (Lost Cause) 2042
Kentucky Culture (Lost Cause) 2040
Kentucky Microcards. Series A. Modern Language Series (Univ of Kentucky Pr) 2041
Kenya National Archives (Kenya Archives) 2037
King, Martin Luther. Assassination File (See 2298)
Knoedler Library on Microfiche (Knoedler) 2050
Labor Research Department. Books and Pamphlets Collection, 1916-1981 (World) 2055
Lambeth Palace Library. [Manuscript Collections] (World) 2060
Lande, Lawrence. Canadiana Collection (See 2113)
Landmarks of Science (Part I) (Readex) 2071
Landmarks of Science II (Readex) 2072
Latin American Documents (General) 2090
Latin American Statistics on Microfiche (IDC) 2100
Latin American Travels (General) 2110
Latin American and Caribbean Official Statistical Serials on Microfiche (Chadwyck-
    Healey) 2080
Law Books Recommended for Libraries (Rothman) 2109
Law Reform Commission of Canada. Working Papers, Study Papers, etc. (Hein) 2111
Law Reprint Series (BNA) 2112
Lawrence Lande Collection of Canadiana. Canadian Historical Documents (Public
    Archives/Canada) 2113
League of Nations Documents and Serial Publications 1919-1946 (RP) 2120
League of Nations and United Nations Treaty Series (LLMC) 2119
Learning Resource System (IHS) 2130
The Left In Britain (Harvester) 2140
Legislative History Service (Microcard/IHS) 2143
Lenin to Khrushchev: The USSR in Retrospect, 1917-1956 (Readex) 2150
Lhasa Kanjur (Inst Adv St Wld Rel) 2168

Library of American Civilization (See 2325)
The Library of American Indian Affairs (See 1900)
A Library of Americana (Lost Cause) 2170
Library of Church Unity Periodicals in Microfilm (Mf Svcs & Sales) 2185
Library of Congress. Cyrillic Union Catalog, 1952-1956 (Readex) 2175
Library of English Literature (See 2326)
Library of Southern Literature (Microcard) 2193
The Library of Thomas Jefferson (Microcard) 2195
Library of the Boreal Institute of Northern Studies (Publisher Unknown) 2187
Library of the Inner Temple. Manuscripts and Early Printed Works (World) 2190
Lincoln Cathedral Library. Seventeenth-Century Pamphlet Collection (World) 2210
Lincoln Cathedral Library. The Mediaeval Manuscript Collection (World) 2200
Listening to Indians (MCA) 2215
The Literature of Folklore (General) 2220
The Literature of Theology and Church History: British Theological Studies (Lost
    Cause) 2230
The Literature of Theology and Church History: Church History in the United States
    of America (Lost Cause) 2231
Little Magazines Series 1889-1972 (World) 2240
Little Magazines on Microfiche (Brookhaven) 2235
London Directories from the Guildhall Library 1677-1855 (RP) 2250
The London Theatre. John Thomas Dibdem (See 1175)
The London Times Intelligence File (MCA) 2260
London Trades Council. Minutes and Papers 1860-1953 (World) 2265
Longe Play Collection (Lib of Congress) 2270
The MAGIC Documents (Univ Pub Am) 2291
Mackenzie Valley Pipeline Inquiry. Briefs and Transcripts of Public Hearings
    (Micromedia) 2280
Maclean-Hunter Vertical Files on Canadian Current Events (See 3660)
The Maclure Collection of French Revolutionary Materials (RP) 2290
Magic (RP) 2292
Major Studies and Issue Briefs of the Congressional Research Service (Univ Pub Am) 2293
Manhattan Project: Official History and Documents (Univ Pub Am) 2294
Manuscripta (St Louis Univ) 2295
Marburger Index: Photographic Documentation of Art in Germany (Bild Foto Marb) 2296
Martene Veterum Scriptorum (Microcard) 2297
Martene, Edmond. Veterum Scriptorum et Monumentorum Historicum (See 2297)
Martin Luther King Assassination File (SRI) 2298
Mazainades 1649-1652 (AMS) 2299
McCarthy Collection of Alcohol Literature (See 2810)
Medical School Information System (See 1940)
Medieval Manuscripts in Microform. Series I. Major Treasures in the Bodleian
    Library (Oxford Microform Pubs) 2311
Medina's Biblioteca Hispano-Americana (General) 2320
Memorial Historico Espanol (See 0008)
Menshevik Collection (Hoover Institution) 2322
Mexican Boundary Commission Papers (Publisher Unknown) 2321
Mexican Culture Series (Publisher Unknown) 2319
Michigan Early Modern English Materials (UMI) 2318
Micro-Miniprints (Hein) 2327
Microbook Library of American Civilization (LRI) 2325
Microbook Library of English Literature (LRI) 2326

Microcard Publications in Music (Univ of Rochester) 2324
Microcard Publications of Primary Records in Culture and Personality (Microcard
   Foundation) 2329
Microfiche College Catalog Collection (Career Guidance Fndn) 2328
Microfiche of Books Listed in Law Books Recommended for Libraries (AALS) (Rothman) 2331
Microfiche of Environmental Impact Statements, 1970 on (Infor Res Press) 2333
Microfilm Archive of Texas Archeology (Council of Tx Archeo) 2340
Microfilm Collection of Confederate Imprints (See 1040)
Microfilm Collection of Manuscripts on American Indian Cultural Anthropology (See 3544)
A Microform Library: Sources for the History of Social Welfare in America
   (Greenwood/CIS) 2350
Microlog (Micromedia) 2360
Micrologue (See 1010)
Middle East Development Documents on Microfiche (IDC) 2370
Middle East: Special Studies, 1970-1980 (Publisher Unknown) 2368
Migne, Jacques Paul. Patrologie Cursus Completas... Series Graeica... Series Latina
   (Microcard) 2375
Mini-Biblex (B & H Montreal) 2377
Missionary Periodicals from the China Mainland (Greenwood/CIS) 2380
Model Cities Reports (MCA) 2395
Modern Indonesia Microfiche Project (IDC) 2397
Monarch Notes (B & H) 2398
Monatschefte Fuer Chemie 21-30 (Microcard) 2398
Monographs of the Society for Research in Child Development (Johnson Associates) 2396
Moravian Church Music Copied By Johannes Herbst (Univ Music Editions) 2399
Morgry, Pierre. Decouvertes et Establissements des Francais dans l'Ouest ... 1879-
   1888 (AMS) 2401
The Mormons and Utah (See 3640)
MusiCache (B & H) 2410
Music Dictionaries and Encyclopedias; Microfiche Reprints of the Major Music Dict
   etc 1475-1900 (Brookhaven) 2400
Musical Americana on Microfilm (Lib of Congress) 2402
Musical Antiquarian Society. Publications (Univ Music Editions) 2403
Musicography in English Translation (U of Kentucky) 2414
Myrdal Collection: The Negro in America, 1938-1943 (Carnegie Corp) 2416
NCJRS Microfiche Program. United States National Criminal Justice Reference Service
   (NCJRS) 2438
The NCR PCMI Library Information System (See 2552)
National Advisory Commission for Aeronautics, 1915-1958 (UPDATA) 2417
National Clearing House on Aging. SCAN Microfiche Collection (See 3028)
National Collection of Watercolors in the Victoria and Albert Museum (Ormonde) 2420
National Criminal Justice Reference Service (NCJRS) (See 2438)
National Development Plans (IDC) 2430
National Portrait Gallery. The Hill Adamson Albums (World) 2427
National Statistical Compendiums (See 1140)
National Woman's Party Papers, 1913-1974 (MCA) 2435
National Woman's Party. Papers: The Suffrage Years, 1913-1020 (MCA) 2436
Native American Legal Materials (LLMC) 2437
Negro Newspaper Microfilm Series (Publisher Unknown) 2452
The Negro: Emancipation to World War I (IHS) 2440
New International Order: Documentation Service on Microfiche (IDC) 2460
New Shakespeare Society, London. Publications. Series 1-8 (Microcard/IHS) 2463

New York Court of Appeals Records and Briefs, 1981- (Hein) 2466
New York Law Journal (B & H) 2464
New York Theatre 1919-1961 (Chadwyck-Healey) 2470
Newberry Library. Chicago. Courtesy Books (See 1290)
Newsbank Urban Affairs Library (Newsbank) 2475
Nicolas de Bonneville et le Cercle Social (Hachette) 2478
Nineteenth Century American Literature on Microcards (Lost Cause) 2489
Nineteenth Century American Literature and History: Ohio Valley and the South (Lost
    Cause) 2490
Nineteenth Century American Literature and History: Trans Mississippi West (Lost
    Cause) 2491
Nineteenth Century English and American Drama (See 1370)
Nineteenth Century Popular British Drama Acting Editions (U of Washington Pr) 2494
Nineteenth Century Russia: Contemporary French Opinion (Hachette) 2500
Nineteenth Century Russian Publicists (See 2920)
Nineteenth and Twentieth Century English and American Drama (General) 2480
The Nixon Administration: A Microfiche Library (Johnson Assoc/NEC) 2503
North America: CO5, Colonial Office, America and the West Indies. Original
    Correspondence (KTO) 2505
North American Indian Collection (Micro Ctr/Texas) 2510
North American Indian Newspapers (See 1060)
North American Indian Periodicals (See 2570)
Northern Ireland Political Literature: Phase I, 1968-72 (Irish Micro) 2521
Northern Ireland Political Literature: Phase II, 1973-75 (Irish Micro) 2522
Northwestern Museum of Science and Industry Collection. See Early Rare Photographic
    Works 2527
Nursing II: A Selected Collection of Academic and Professional Nursing Materials
    (UMI) 2528
O.S.S./State Department Intelligence and Research Reports (Univ Pub Am) 2540
OECE Publications (OECD) 2536
Oberlin College Collection of Anti-Slavery Propaganda Pamphlets (See 0380)
Official Records of the Union and Confederate Armies. ... Navies (National
    Archives) 2531
Ohio State Supreme Court Records and Briefs (Microcard/Hein) 2529
The Oneida Community Collection in Syracuse University Library (MCA) 2532
Onteris (Publisher Unknown) 2534
Opera Librettos Printed Before 1800 (Lib of Congress) 2533
Oregon. University. School of Health, Physical Education and Recreation (See 1740)
Organization of American States. Documentos Oficiales/Official Documents (OAS) 2535
Oxford Music School Collection at the Bodleian Library (Harvester) 2545
PCMI Ultrafiche Library Collections (Microlection/NCR) 2552
Pamphlets in American History (MCA) 2550
Pamphlets in the Public Archives of Canada (See 0800)
Panama Canal Studies (Lib of Congress) 2549
Papers of Alexander H. Stephens (Lib of Congress) 2548
Papers of Benjamin Henry Latrobe (Md Hist Soc/JT White) 2554
Papers of the Americans for Democratic Action (MCA) 2556
Papers of the Congress for Racial Equality, 1941-1967 (MCA) 2557
Papers of the Pennsylvania Abolitionist Society (Rhistoric Pub) 2551
Papyrology on Microfiche (See 0295)
The Parliamentary History of England From the Earliest Period to the Year 1803
    (Publisher Unknown) 2555

Patrologaiae Cursus Completus (See 2375)
Peabody Catalog II (Microcard) 2553
Pedagogic Theory in 18th Century France (Hachette) 2558
Peel Bibliography on Microfiche (Bibliography of the Prairie Provinces to 1953)
   (Nat Lib Canada) 2560
Pennsylvania Abolitionist Society. Papers (See 2551)
Pennsylvania Newspapers (Microsurance) 2566
Pennsylvania Side Reports (Publisher Unknown) 2565
Percy Society. Early English Poetry, Ballads and Popular Literature of the Middle
   Ages (Microcard) 2568
Periodicals By and About North American Indians (MCA) 2570
Periodicals in Musicology (Research Micro Pub) 2572
Personal Sources for the History of Russia (See 2930)
Perspectives in Acculturation: Miscellaneous Studies of Canada's Native Peoples
   (Publisher Unknown) 2573
Phelps-Stokes Fellowship Papers (Univ of Virginia) 2575
Philippine Culture Series (Microcard) 2577
Phonefiche (B & H) 2580
Photographic Views of New York City, 1870's-1970's (UMI) 2590
Pickett Papers (See 2811)
Pierce, Charles Sanders (See 0931)
Place Papers in the British Library (See 2760)
The Plains and the Rockies (Lost Cause) 2600
Playbills 1958-1975 (Greenwood/CIS) 2620
Playbills from the Harvard Theatre Collection (RP) 2610
Poe, Alexander. Collection in the University of Virginia Library (See 2023)
Politics and Administration of Tudor and Stuart England (Harvester) 2630
Pollard, Alfred W. Early English Books (See 1281)
Portraits of Americans (Chadwyck-Healey) 2640
Portuguese Books Before 1601 (See 1760)
Prairie Provinces, Bibliography (See 2560)
Pre-1865 English Law Reports (Trans Media) 2643
Presbyterian Historical Society. Collection of Missionaries Letters (See 0190)
Presidential Documents Series (Univ Pub Am) 2648
Presidential Election Campaign Biographies 1824-1972 (UMI) 2650
Presidential Papers Microfilms (Lib of Congress) 2652
Press Conferences of the Secretaries of State, 1922-1974 (Publisher Unknown) 2654
Primary Records in Culture and Personality (See 2329)
Prince Society. Publications (Microcard) 2653
Proceedings of the Society of Plastics Industries of Canada, 33rd-35th, 1976, 1977,
   1979 (Nash Inf Svcs) 2655
Profile: Canadian Provincial Government Publications on Microfiche (Micromedia) 2660
Project South: Oral History Collection of Stanford University (See 3225)
Public Order, Discontent, and Protest in 19th Century England 1820-1850 (PRO Class
   H052) (Harvester) 2670
Public Records of Great Britain, Series 1-4 (Publisher Unknown) 2675
Publicat: A Canadian Federal Documents Service (Micromedia) 2680
The Publications of the English Record Societies 1835-1970 (Chadwyck-Healey) 2691
Publications of the Henry Bradshaw Society (Slangenburg Abb) 2685
Published Colonial Records of the American Colonies (RP) 2700
Publishers' Archives on Microfilm (See 0744)
Quaker Manuscripts Collection: Phase A (World) 2705

Quaker Women's Diaries (World) 2707

Queen's College, Cambridge. The Mediaeval Manuscript Collection (World) 2710

RIDIM: Repertoire International d'Iconographie Musicale (IDC) 2870

Radical Pamphlet Literature: A Collection from the Tamiment Library 1817-1970 (MCA) 2720

Radical Periodicals in the United States, 1880-1960 (Greenwood/CIS) 2730

Radical Periodicals of Great Britain 1794-1950 (Greenwood/CIS) 2740

Radical Politics and the Working Man in England: The Papers of Francis Place in the British Library (Harvester) 2760

Radical Reformation Microfiche Project (IDC) 2770

The Radical Right and Patriotic Movements in Britain (Harvester) 2780

Rare Militant British 19th Century Freethought Books (World) 2790

Rare Nineteenth Century American Art Journals (Earl M Coleman Ent) 2795

Rare Radical and Labour Periodicals of Great Britain in the Nineteenth Century (Harvester) 2800

Rawlinson Collection. Bodleian Library, Oxford (See 3100)

Raymond G. McCarthy Memorial Collection of Alcohol Literature (Kraus/Johnson) 2810

Recherche en histoire sociale (Hachette) 2809

Records of the Church of England During the Commonwealth Period, 1643-61 (World) 2814

Records of the Confederate States of America (Lib of Congress) 2811

Records of the States of the United States (Lib of Congress) 2813

Redgrave, Gilbert. Early English Books (See 1281)

Reform of Local Government Structures in the United States 1945-1971 (Kraus/Johnson) 2820

La Reforme de l'enseignement au Siecle des Lumieres (Hachette) 2821

Reformed Protestantism (H. Bullinger and the Surcher Reformation) (IDC) 2822

Regional History of Business in the Southwest, No. 1-14, Univ of Texas (MCA) 2823

Rehabilitation and Handicapped Literature, 1950 on (MCA) 2825

Religion in America (UMI) 2830

Repertoire International d'Iconographie Musicale (See 2870)

Reports of Corporations Filed With the Securities and Exchange Commission (See 1190)

Reports of Explorations Printed in the Documents of the United States Government (RP) 2840

Reprints of Texas History (Micro Ctr/Texas) 2845

Rerum Britannicarum Medii Aevi Scriptores (See 1703)

Research Reports of Ontario Ministry of Education (Publisher Unknown) 2847

Restoration History Microfiche Library (Daystar Micropub) 2749

Reverse Discrimination and the Supreme Court: A Microfiche Collection of Records and Briefs (IHS) 2848

Revistas Hispano-Americanos (General) 2846

Rhoda Kellog Child Art Collection (IHS) 2850

Rhodes Collection (National Archives) 2858

The Rhodes House Library, Oxford. Anti-Slavery Collection (World) 2860

The Richardson Collection (UMI:UK) 2867

Right Wing Collection of the University of Iowa Libraries (MCA) 2880

The Rolls Series. (Rerum Britannicarum Medii Aevi Scriptores) (Microcard) 1703

Rosenbach, A.S.W. Early American Children's Books (Kraus) 2890

Le Rousseauisme (Hachette) 2895

Roxburghe Club of London. Publications (Lib of Congress) 2906

Royal Archives at Windsor Castle. Victorian Photographic Collection (World) 2900

Royal Commission on Historical Monuments (England), 1910-1972 (Chadwyck-Healey) 2901

Royal Commissions in Canada (See 1480)

Royal Institute of British Architects. Architectural Treatises and Works on Perspective (World) 2903

Royal Institute of British Architects. English Pattern Books (World) 2904

Royal Institute of British Architects. Rare Book Collection (World) 2905
Russia. Censorship in Tsarist Russia (IDC) 2910
Russia. Nineteenth-Century Russian Publicists (IDC) 2920
Russia. Personal Sources for the History of Russia in the Nineteenth Century (IDC) 2930
Russian Books Printed in Moscow in the 16th and 17th Centuries (See 2690)
Russian Books before 1701 (General) 2690
Russian Culture Series 1800-1917 (General) 2970
Russian Futurism, 1910-1916, Poetry and Manifestoes (Chadwyck-Healey) 2975
Russian Historical Sources: First Series (Readex) 2991
Russian Historical Sources: Second Series (Readex) 2992
Russian History and Culture (UMI) 3000
Russian Publications, Eighteenth Century (General) 3010
Russian Revolutionary Literature (RP) 3020
Russian and Eastern European Resource Material: Collections (Lib Microfilms) 2940
Russian and Soviet Law, Including Foreign and International Law: Microfiche Project
    (IDC) 2950
La Russie et l'Opinion Francaise au 19e Siecle (See 2500)
SCAN-National Clearinghouse on Aging. Service Center for Aging Information.
    Microfiche Collection (SCAN) 3028
SDS Papers (MCA) 3061
SPCK Early 18th Century Archives (World) 3215
SRI Microfiche Library (Statistical Reference Index) (CIS) 3220
Sabin, Joseph. Biblioteca Americana (See 3060)
Saccardo, Pier Andrea. Syllage Fungorum Huscusque Cognitorum (Microcard) 3021
Sahel: Documents and Dissertations (UMI) 3024
Les Saint-Sinomiens, 1825-1834 (Hachette) 3023
Scandinavian Culture Series (General) 3030
Scherer Collection (See 1650)
Schomburg Center for Research in Black Culture: A Selection from the Schomburg
    Center: I (Kraus) 3040
Schomburg Center for Research in Black Culture: A Selection from the Schomburg
    Center: II (Kraus/3M) 3042
Science Fiction Periodicals Series I: 1926-1945 (Greenwood/CIS) 3051
Science Fiction Periodicals Series II (Greenwood/CIS) 3052
Science Societies (Microcard) 3053
Scientific Journals, 17th Century on (Readex) 3054
Scottish Text Society. Publications (Microcard) 3057
A Select Collection of Old English Plays (See 1198)
Selected Americana from Sabin's Dictionary of Books Relating to America (Lost Cause) 3060
Selection de Journaux Ephemeres, 1869-1871 (ACRPP) 3064
Selection de Journaux Ephemeres, 1848-1850 (ACRPP) 3065
Selection de Journaux Ephemeres de la Periode de la Revolution (ACRPP) 3066
Session Laws of American States and Territories (Hein/UMI/IHS) 3062
Sessional Papers. Great Britain. Parliament (See 1695-1699)
Seventeenth and Eighteenth Century Periodicals and Academy Publications (RP) 3070
Sexual Politics in Britain (Harvester) 3090
The Shaker Collection of the Western Reserve Historical Society (MCA) 3093
Shakespeare Society (New). Publications (See 2463)
Shakespeare Society. Publications (Microcard) 3095
Shakespeare-Jahrbach (Microcard) 3096
Shaw, Ralph R. Early American Imprints (See 1232)
Shobutsu Ruisan, 1738-1747 (Yushodo) 3098

Shoemaker, Richard H. Early American Imprints (See 1232)
Short-Title Catalog (See 1281/1282)
Sibley Music Library. Eastman School of Music. University of Rochester (Univ of
    Rochester) 3099
Sixteenth and Seventeenth Century MSS from the Rawlinson Collection in the Bodleian
    Library, Oxford (Harvester) 3100
Slave Narratives. Federal Writers Project (Lib of Cong/Andr) 3103
Slavery (MCA) 3105
Slavery Source Materials (IHS) 3120
Slavery and Anti-Slavery Pamphlets From the Libraries of Salmon P. Chase and John
    P. Hale (UMI) 3107
Slavery: Source Material and Critical Literature (Lost Cause) 3110
Slavic Palaeography (IDC) 3140
Smithsonian Publications Relating to the North American Indian (MCA) 3145
Social Problems and the Churches: The Harlan Paul Douglass Collection of Religious
    Research Projects (RP) 3160
Social Welfare in America (See 2350)
Social and Economic Development Plans (See also 2430) (IDC) 3150
Socialist Collections in the Tamiment Library, 1872-1956 (MCA) 3163
Societe des Anciens Textes Francais. Publications (See 3165)
Society of Ancient French Texts. Publications (Microcard) 3165
Sorciers, Demonologues, Magistrats, Theologiens et Medicins aus XVIe et XVIIe
    Siecles (Hachette) 3170
Sotheby Catalogs (UMI) 3175
Source Materials Relating to the Struggle for American Independence (See 0290)
Source Materials in the Field of Theatre (UMI) 3180
Sources Statistiques de l'Histoire de France (Hachette) 3183
Sources for the History of Social Welfare in America (See 2350)
South Africa. Treason Trials (South Africa) 3196
South Africa: A Collection of Political Documents Covering the Years 1902-1963
    (Hoover Institution) 3194
South Asian Art (IDC) 3190
South Carolina Newspapers, 1732-1782 (Charlst Lib Soc) 3195
Southeast Asian Theses Project (Manila Univ Lib) 3198
Southern Historical Manuscripts: Plantation Records, 1748-1901 (Greenwood) 3199
Southern Tenant Farmers' Union. Papers, 1934-1970 (MCA) 3197
Soviet and Communist Party Press: A Collection of Historical and Documentary
    Studies on Microfilm (Bay) 3201
Sowerby's Catalog of the Library of Thomas Jefferson (See 2195)
Spanish Books Before 1601 (See 1760)
Spanish Drama (General) 3200
Spanish Drama of the Golden Age: The Comedia Collection of the U of Pennsylvania
    Libraries (RP) 3210
Spanish and Portuguese Bibliographies, Catalogs and Indexes (Readex) 3213
Species, Genera et Ordines Algarum (See 0085)
Stanford University Project. South Oral History Collection (MCA) 3225
Stanford University. Hoover Institution on War, Revolution, and Peace. Menshevik
    Collection (See 2322)
State Censuses (Kraus) 3230
State Constitutional Conventions, Commissions, and Amendments on Microfiche
    (Greenwood/CIS) 3235
State Labor Proceedings 1885-1974 (Greenwood/CIS) 3240

State Publications Service (IHS) 3250
State Reports Prior to the National Reporter System (Trans Media) 3265
State Reports on Correction and Punishment, Poverty and Public Welfare, Prior to
    1930 (Kraus/Redgrave) 3260
State Session Laws (See 3062)
Statistics Canada Publications 1851- (Micromedia) 3270
Stephens, Alexander H. Papers (See 2550)
Stevens. B.F. Facsimiles of Manuscripts in European Archives Relating to America (See 0528)
Strategie et Art de la Grande Guerre (Hachette) 3275
Structures Sociales Sous l'Ancien Regime (Hachette) 3278
Sung Chi-Sha Tsang (Inst Adv St Wld Rel) 3274
Survey of the Conditions of the Indians in the United States (Publisher Unknown) 3279
Sutro Library Mexican Pamphlet Collection (Cal St Lib. Sutro Br) 3277
Svodnyi Katalog Russkoi Knigi XVIII v (See 3010)
Syracuse University. The Oneida Community Collection (See 2532)
Tamiment Library. Socialist Collections, 1872-1956 (See 3163)
Tanganyika National Archives (Publisher Unknown) 3285
Tests in Microfiche (Educ Testing S) 3290
Texas as Province and Republic, 1795-1845 (RP) 3295
Theater Playbills From the Harvard Theater Collection (Publisher Unknown) 3298
Le Theatre de la Revolution et de l'Empire (Clearwater) 3300
Theology and the History of Religion (Lost Cause) 3310
Third Party Presidential Nominating Proceedings, 1830-1868 (Northern Microgr) 3313
The Thomason Tracts: The Pamphlets, Books, Newspapers, and MSS Collected by Geo
    Thomason, 1640-1661 (UMI) 3315
Three Centuries of Drama (See 3320)
Three Centuries of English and American Plays 1500-1830 (Readex) 3320
Three Centuries of French Drama (General) 3330
Tibetan Religious Works: PL480 and SFC Collections (Inst Adv St Wld Rel) 3335
Toronto Public Library. Canadiana (See 0910)
Traite, Esclavage et Contestage en France (Hachette) 3337
Traites d'Architecture, XVIe-XIXe Siecles (Hachette) 3340
Transportation Masterfile 1921-1971 (HDI) 3360
Travel Literature. Series I. The Americas (Louisville/Falls Cit) 3368
Travels in the Confederate States (Lost Cause) 3370
Travels in the Near and Middle East (General) 3380
Travels in the New South I, Thomas D. Clark (Lost Cause) 3390
Travels in the New South II: Thomas D. Clark (Lost Cause) 3391
Travels in the Old South I (Lost Cause) 3400
Travels in the Old South II (Lost Cause) 3402
Travels in the Old South III (Lost Cause) 3403
Travels in the West, Southwest and Northwest (Lost Cause) 3410
Trigant Burrow Research Collection (RP) 3413
Trinity College, Cambridge, Library. The Mediaeval Manuscript Collection (World) 3430
Twaites, Reuben Gold. Early Western Travels, 1748-1846 (Microcard) 3415
The Twentieth-Century Trade Union Woman (MCA/NYT Oral Hist) 3423
The Ultra Documents (Clearwater) 3440
Ultrafiche Library Collections (See 2552)
Underground Newspapers Microfilm Collection (See 3460)
Underground Press Collection (B & H) 3460
The Underground and Alternative Press in Britain 1961-1972; 1973- (Harvester) 3450
United Nations Documents and Official Records from 1946 to the Present (Readex) 3470

United States Bureau of Mines Collection, 1910 on (UPDATA) 3472
United States Census Publications in Microform 1820-1967 (CIS/Greenwood) 3475
United States Congress. American State Papers 1789-1838; Serial Set 15th Congress
  1817 onward (See 3545)
United States Congressional Committee Hearings on Microfiche: Early 1800's through
  1969 (CIS/Greenwood) 3485
United States Congressional Committee Prints on Microfiche, Retrospective through
  1969 (CIS/Greenwood) 3486
United States Congressional Hearings and Committee Prints, 1956 on (Readex) 3487
United States Government Bibliography Masterfile 1924-1973 (Carrollton) 3500
United States Government Documents (LLMC) (LLMC) 3503
United States Government Periodicals. 1975- (MCA) 3505
United States Government Publications: Depository Publications 1956- (Readex) 3510
United States Government Publications: Non-Depository Publications 1953- (Readex) 3511
United States Government Publications: Select Agency Publications (Readex) 3513
United States Joint Publications Research Service (JPRS) Reports (Readex) 3520
United States National Technical Information Service. SRIM (Selected Reports in
  Microfiche) (NTIS) 3530
United States Serial Set (1817 to Present) and American State Papers (1789-1838)
  (Readex) 3545
United States State Documents (General) 3547
United States. Advisory Commission on Intergovernmental Relations. Policy Reports
  (PDF) 3471
United States. American State Papers. CIS (See 0980)
United States. Army. Mathematics Research Center. MRC Technical Reports (MRC) 3469
United States. Army. Military History Research Collection. Camp Newspapers (USAMHRC) 3473
United States. Bureau of American Ethnology. Bulletin (Microcard) 3476
United States. Bureau of Indian Affairs. Annual Reports (See 0775)
United States. Bureau of the Census. 1st-10th Census, 1790-1880. Population
  Schedules (National Archives) 3474
United States. Congress. Congressional Globe (Princeton Microfilm) 3481
United States. Congress. Debates and Proceedings (Microcard) 3482
United States. Decennial Census Publications (RP) 3491
United States. Department of State. Records Relating to Internal Affairs, 1910-1929
  (National Archives) 2812
United States. Department of State. Consular Instructions (Publisher Unknown) 3488
United States. Department of State. Foreign Relations (Microcard) 3489
United States. Dept of War. Official Records of the Union and Confederate Armies
  ... Navies (See 2531)
United States. Dept. of Energy. Reports on Research (Publisher Unknown) 3492
United States. Educational Resources Information Center (See 1455)
United States. Federal Register, 1944-1974 (Brookhaven) 3483
United States. Foreign Broadcast Information Service. Daily Reports (Lib of Congress) 3522
United States. Historic American Buildings Survey (See 1771)
United States. Immigration Commission. Reports. 1907-1910 (See 1873)
United States. Indian Claims Commission (See 1900)
United States. Joint Publications Research Service (NTIS) 3521
United States. Laws, Statutes, Etc. United States Statutes at Large (Microcard) 3523
United States. Library of Congress. Congressional Research Service. Major Studies
  and Issue Briefs (See 2293)
United States. Library of Congress et al. National Program for Acquisitions and
  Cataloging (NPAC). Jakarta (Lib of Congr et al) 3524

United States. National Advisory Committee on Aeronautics Materials on Microfiche
(Publisher Unknown) 3526
United States. National Aeronautics and Space Administration Materials on
Microfiche (Publisher Unknown) 3527
United States. National Archives. Returns From Military Posts (Publisher Unknown) 3525
United States. National Clearing House on Aging (See 3028)
United States. National Criminal Justice Reference Service (See 2438)
United States. Serial Set. CIS (See 0980)
United States. Supreme Court. Records and Briefs (BNA/IHS/UMI) 3546
University Music Editions. Microfiche Reprint Series (High Density) 3549
University of Chicago Library. Microfilm Collection of Manuscripts on American
Indian Cultural Anthropology (Univ of Chicago Lib) 3544
University of Pennsylvania Indic Manuscripts (Inst Adv St Wld Rel) 3552
University of Rochester Press. Canadian Studies Series (Publisher Unknown) 3551
University of South Dakota. Indian Oral History Collection (Publisher Unknown) 3553
University of Texas, Austin. Bexar Archives (See 0533)
Unpublished Manuscripts from the Great English Collections (Harvester) 3548
Unpublished State Papers of the English Civil War and Interregnum 1642-1660
(Harvester) 3550
Urban Canada/Canada Urbain (Micromedia) 3570
Urban Documents Microfiche Collection (Greenwood/CIS) 3580
Urban and Rural Social Conditions in Industrial Britian (Harvester) 3560
Utah and the Mormons (RP) 3640
Utopian Literature, Pre-1900 Imprints (MCA) 3645
Utopies au Siecle des Lumieres (Hachette) 3646
Valazquez, Gonzolo. Biblioteca de obras puertorriqueno (NYPL) 3650
Vandamm Collection. New York Theatre (See 2470)
Vertical Files (Maclean-Hunter) 3660
Victoria and Albert Museum Photographic Collection (Mindata) 3680
Victorian Fiction (General) 3690
Victorian Fiction and Other Nineteenth Century Fiction (See 3690)
Victorian Philanthropy and Social Problems (Harvester) 3700
Victorian Photographic Collection (See 2900)
Visual Union Catalog of Miniatures in Great Britain (Emmett) 3710
Vital Speeches of the Day (UMI) 3712
Voltaire, Francois. Oeuvres Completes de Voltaire (Microcard) 3714
Voyageurs en Mediterranee, XVI-XVIIIe (Hachette) 3713
War in Vietnam: Histories by the NSC Transcripts and Files of the Paris Peace Talks
on Vietnam, 1968-1973 (Publisher Unknown) 3715
Western Americana (UMI) 3720
Western Americana: Frontier History of the Trans-Mississippi West 1550-1900 (RP) 3730
Western European Census Reports 1960 (Kraus/Redgrave) 3740
William S. Gray Research Collection in Reading (A T Burrows Ins) 3750
Winchester College (Warden & Fellows' Library): Mediaeval Manuscripts Collection
(World) 3770
Wing, Donald G. Early English Books (See 1282)
Wisconsin. State Historical Society. Draper Manuscripts (See 1203)
Witchcraft in Europe and America (RP) 3780
Witness Index to the United States Congressional Hearings 25th-89th Congress (1839-
1966) (CIS/Greenwood) 3790
Wolfenbuttel. Herzog August Bibliothek. Libretti (Kraus) 3800
Women and Health/Mental Health (Women's Hist RC) 3810

Women and Law (Women's Hist RC) 3820
Women's History Collection. Herstory (See 1750)
Women's History Research Center. Library (See 1750/3810/3820)
Women's History. The Gerritsen Collection (See 1660)
Women's Rights Pamphlets. Cornell University (See 1080)
Women's Rights: Source Materials Relating to Woman's March Toward Equality (IHS) 3840
Woodwind Instruction Books, 1600-1830 (Lib of Congress) 3843
World Council of Churches. Faith and Order Commission. Official Pamphlets and
    Publications (Tex Christ Univ) 3845
Wright, Lyle H. American Fiction (See 0151/0152/0160)
Writings of Daniel Defoe (UMI) 3855
Yab Sras Gsuns 'bum (Inst Adv St/Wrld Rel) 3857
Yale Collection of German Baroque Literature (See 1622)
Yiddish Classics on Microfiche (Clearwater) 3860
Youth, Law, and Justice (MCA) 3865
Zeitschrift fur Englische Philogie (See 0335)

List of Publishers

This list gives the full names of publishers that are referred to in compressed form within this Appendix and those that follow. Additional information may be found in <u>Microform Market Place</u> (Meckler Publishing, Westport, CT) or other publisher and information industry directories. Where known, city and state have been given for publishers not listed in MMP.

A T Burrows Ins - Alvina Treut Burrows Institute
Am Micro-Data - American Micro-Data
Americana Unlim - Americana Unlimited
B & H - Bell & Howell Micro Photo Division
Bild Photo Marb - Bildarchiv Foto Marburg
CIHM - Canadian Institute for Historical Microfiche
Chadwyck-H/MRI - Chadwyck-Healey/Microform Review Inc
Charlst Lib Soc - Charleston Library Society, Charleston, S.C.
Clearwater - Clearwater Publishing Inc
Ctr Rech Hist - Centre de Recherche en Histoire Economique du Canada
        Francais, Montreal
EIC - Environment Information Center
EP - EP is now Microform Limited
Ecum Res Agency - Ecumenism Research Agency, Estes Park, CO
Educ Testing S - Educational Testing Service
Fearon Pitman - Fearon Reference Systems, a Division of Pitman Learning Inc
France Expans - France-Expansion
General - General Microfilm Co
Godfrey - Godfrey Memorial Library
Greenwood - Greenwood Press, a Division of Congressional Information
        Service Inc
HDI - The United States Historical Documents Institute
Harvard Law S L - Harvard Law School Library Microform Project
Harvester - Harvester Microform Publications Ltd
Human Rel Ar F - Human Relations Area Files
IDC - Inter Documentation Company AG
IHS - Information Handling Services
Infor Res Press - Information Resources Press
Irish Micro - Irish Microforms Ltd
Knoedler - M. Knoedler and Co Inc
Kraus - Kraus Microform
LRI - Library Resources Inc
Lib Microfilms - Library Microfilms
Lib of Congress - Library of Congress Photoduplication Service
Lost Cause - Lost Cause Press
MCA - Microfilming Corporation of America
MIMC - Microforms International Marketing Corp, a subsidiary of Pergamon
        Press, Inc
Maclean-Hunter - Maclean-Hunter Micropublishing Co
Mf Svcs & Sales - Microfilm Service and Sales Co, Dallas, TX

Micro Ctr/Texas - Microfilm Center Inc
Micro Hachette - Microeditions Hachette
Micromedia- Micromedia Limited
NTIS - National Technical Information Service
Nash Inf Svcs - Nash Information Services, formerly Mary Nash Information
     Services
Nat Gal Canada - National Gallery of Canada
Nat Lib Canada - National Library of Canada
Nat Micro Lib - National Microfilm Library, Career Guidance Foundation,
     College Catalog Library
OAS - Organization of American States
Oxford Microf - Oxford Microform Publications
POF/Clearwater - Publications Orietalistes de France/Clearwater
     Publishing Inc
Pub Arc/Canada - Public Archives of Canada
RP - Research Publications, Inc
Readex - Readex Microprint Corp
Rothman - Fred B. Rothman & Co
St Louis Univ - St Louis University, Pius XII Library, Vatican Film
     Library
Tex Christ Univ - Texas Christian University
U of Chicago Pr - University of Chicago Press
U of Oregon - University of Oregon, College of Health, Physical Education
     and Recreation-Microform Publications
UMI - University Microfilms International
UPDATA - UPDATA Publications Inc
Univ Pub Am - University Publications of America Inc
Women's Hist RC - Women's History Research Center
World - World Microfilms Publications Ltd

Appendix E

Microform Sets That Are Not Represented in the Clearinghouse Data Base

Although these 35 sets were included in the list of sets that accompanied the survey questionnaire, no respondents reported holding them and data for them are consequently not available in the clearinghouse data base. The absense of reports for them does not necessarily mean that few, if any, U.S. or Canadian libraries now hold them. Some sets were newly published at the time the survey was conducted and for that reason had not found their way into libraries. Others may be known in libraries by names so different from those used by their publishers that the connection between the publisher-name and the library-name cannot be made. (These, of course, will be found in the data base under the names that the reporting libraries used in citing them.)

The introduction to Appendix D given information on the form of title used here. Like the list given in Appendix D, this list includes abbreviated publisher names (in parentheses) and the four-digit numbers that are used to identify sets in the survey data base.

The Anarchist Press in Britain (Harvester) - 0320
Archives of the Royal Literary Fund (World) - 0457
Assyriology-Egyptology: Rare Serials and Books on Microfiche (IDC) - 0520
British Theses Relating to British History 1688-1715 (EP) - 0760
Contemporary Culture and Communications: TV and Radio Broadcasting 1927-1976 (Harvester) - 1050
Cox Collection (Lib Microfilms) - 1100
Early Photography Books (Clearwater) - 1310
English Historical Pamphlets (Brookhaven) - 1410
Les Femmes (Clearwater) - 1490
History of Economics: References in Wealth of Nations, Classical Economic Titles, Malthus's Library (MIMC) - 1775
History of Education in the 19th Century (EP) - 1780
History of France (MIMC) - 1785
The Immigrant in America (RP) - 1870
International Labor Office. Reports and Records of Proceedings 1919-81 and continuation (World) - 1968
Micro-Urba (Micro-Urba) - 2323
Napoleon (MIMC) - 2415
Negro Collection (Micro Ctr/Texas) - 2450
New York Listing Applications (MIMC) - 2465
One Hundred Outstanding Illustrated Books (Chadwyck-Healey) - 2530
Radical Periodicals Series 1813-1976 and Continuation (World) - 2750
Records Relating to Australia. 1. The Papers of Antony Gibbs & Sons 1853-1930 (World) - 2815

Records Relating to Australia. 2. The Records of the Corporation of London Records
    Office 1791-1854 (World) - 2816
Russian Historical Series (Harvester) - 2980
Salem Witchcraft Hysteria (B & H) - 3025
Sex Research: Early Literature from Statistics to Erotica (RP) - 3080
Slavery Tracts and Pamphlets from the West India Committee Collection
    (World) - 3130
Symbolism - Futurism - Acmeism - Imagism (IDC) - 3280
Travels in the Near and Middle East (General) - 3380
Twentieth-Century Religious Periodicals (World) - 3420
Victoria and Albert Museum. Early Rare Photographic Collection (World) - 3670
Virgiliana Collection (MIMC) - 3705
The William Smeal Collection. From Glasgow Public Library (World) - 3760
Winchester College (Warden & Fellows' Library): The Collection of 17 & 18th
    Century Manuscripts (World) - 3771
Women in America 1800-1860 (Brookhaven) - 3830
World Exploration (General) - 3850

Appendix F

Microform Sets Cataloged on One or More Bibliographic Utilities

This list shows microform sets for which cataloging is available on one or more of the North American bibliographic utilities. It includes sets that have been fully cataloged as well as ones that are in the process of being cataloged. Titles are listed alphabetically, capital letters before lower-case ones. (Thus JSAJ appears before Jeffersonian Americana.)

Like Appendixes D and E, the list gives set titles, publishers, and four-digit numbers. In addition, it has notations to show whether cataloging is complete or in process and it gives the initial letter of the utility (or utilities) on which the cataloging may be found.

Complete cataloging is indicated by the notation "100%". The phrase "In Progress" is used in two cases where cataloging is in progress: (1) where sets are being acquired on subscription or standing order and (2) where they are held in complete form, but are being cataloged retrospectively.

The letter identifying the utility is given after a diagonal slash. "O" stands for OCLC; "R" for RLIN; "U" for UTLAS; and "W" for WLN. Cataloging on in-house systems is identified only where reports show no entry of records into a bibliographic utility.

ABA Section Proceedings (Atlas Microfilming) 0004-100%/O
ACIR, Collected Publications of the U.S. Advisory Commission on Intergovernmental
   Relations on Microfiche (PDF) 0005-In Progress/W
Adelaide Nutting History Nursing Collection from the History of Nursing Collection,
   Teachers College, Columbia University (UMI) 0018-In Progress/O
Administrative Histories of U.S. Civilian Agencies: Korean War (RP) 0020-100%?/O
Administrative Histories of U.S. Civilian Agencies: World War II (RP) 0030-100%?/O
African Library (Hachette) 0050-In Progress(?)/U
African Official Statistical Serials (Chadwyck-Healey) 0060-In Progress/O
Afro-American Rare Book Collection (Kistler) 0075-100%/O
Agrarian Periodicals in the United States 1920-1960 (Greenwood/CIS) 0090-100%/O
America 1935-1946 (Chadwyck-Healey) 0110-100%?/O
American Architectural Books (RP) 0120-100%/O
American Civil Liberties Union Records and Publications (MCA) 0015-In Progress/O
American Culture: Series I, 1493-1806 (UMI) 0141-In Progress/O
American Culture: Series II, 1493-1875 (UMI) 0142-In Progress/O
American Fiction 1774-1900 (RP) 0151-In Progress/O [Set Processing]
American Fiction 1901-1910 (RP) 0152-In Progress/O [Set Processing]
The American Film Institute Seminars: Part I (MCA) 0181-100%/O
The American Film Institute/Louis B. Mayer Oral History Collection: Part I (MCA)
   0171-100%/O
The American Film Institute/Louis B. Mayer Oral History Collection: Part II (MCA)
   0172-In Progress/O

American Indian Periodicals in the Princeton University Library (Clearwater) 0200-
    100%/O, In Progress/R
American Literary Annuals and Gift Books 1825-1865 (RP) 0220-100%/O
American Natural History (RP) 0230-In Progress/In House System
American Periodicals: Series I, 18th Century (UMI) 0261-100%/O & R
American Periodicals: Series II, 1800-1850 (UMI) 0262-In Progress/O & R
American Periodicals: Series III, 1850-1900 (UMI) 0263-In Progress/O & R
American Society of Papyrologists. Papyrology on Microfiche. Series 1-2 (Am Soc
    Papyrologists) 0295-In Progress/O
American State Papers 1789-1838 (Brookhaven) 0300-In Progress/O
American State Reports Prior to the National Reporter System (Trans Media) 0305-
    In Progress/O
Ancient Roman Architecture (Clearwater) 0330-100%/O
Annual Reports of Major American Corporations (MIMC) 0358-In Progress/O
Archaeological Survey of Canada. Papers. [Commission archaeologique du Canada.
    Dossier.] (Micromedia) 0381-100%/U
Archives Canada Microfiches (Pub Arc/Canada) 0410-In Progress/U
Archives de la Linguistique Francaise: Collection de Documents Relatifs a la Langue
    Francaise 1500-1900 (France Expans) 0420-In Progress/U
Archives of American Publishers (Chadwyck-Healey) 0430-100%/O
The Archives of British Publishers on Microfilm (Chadwyck-Healey) 0440-100%/O
Art Exhibition Catalogues on Microfiche (Chadwyck-Healey) 0470-In Progress/O & U
Attorney General Reports and Opinions (Trans Media) 0527-In Progress/O
B.F. Stevens's Facsimiles of Manuscripts in European Archives Relating to America,
    1773-1783 (AMS) 0528-100%/O
Black Journals: Phase I (Greenwood/CIS) 0543-100%/R
Black Journals: Phase II (Greenwood/CIS) 0544-100%/R
Books About North American Indians on Microfilm (MCA) 0560-100%/O
Books for College Libraries (IHS) 0570-In Progress/W & O
British Periodicals in the Creative Arts (UMI) 0740-In Progress/O
British Records relating to America in Microform (EP) 0750-In Progress/O & R
British Trade Union History Collection (World) 0770-100%/O
A Business History Collection on Microfiche (RP) 0780-100%/O
Camden Society. London. Publications (Microcard/AMS) 0786-100%/U
Camden Society. London. Publications. New Series (Microcard/AMS) 0787-100%/U
Canada Labour Papers on Microfilm in the Labour Canada Library (Pub Arc/Canada)
    0815-In Progress/In House System
Canadian Institute for Historical Micro-Reproduction: Microfiche Collection (CIHM)
    0860-In Progress/U & O
Canadian Newspapers on Microfilm (CLA) 0870-In Progress(?)/U
Canadian Parliamentary Proceedings and Sessional Papers 1841-1970 (HDI)
    0880-In Progress/System Labelled "Other" (GEAC?)
Canadian Theses on Microfiche (Nat Lib Canada) 0893-In Progress/U
Canadiana (Staton and Boyle) (IHS) 0910-In Progress/U
Chaucer Society, London. Publications. Series 1-2 (Microcard) 0932-In Progress/O,
    -100%/R
Chicago Visual Library. Text-Fiche Publications (U of Chicago Pr) 0935-In
    Progress/O, U, & R
Civil War 1861-1865 (MCA) 0995-In Progress/O
Classics of International Law (Trans Media) 0996-100%/O
Code of Federal Regulations (Oceana) 0994-In Progress/O

Appendix F -- Sets Cataloged on One or More Bibliographic Utilities

Coleccion de Documentos Ineditos: 1) Para la Historia de Espana, 2) Relativos al Descubrimiento ... America y Oceania (Microcard) 0997-100%/U

Collection de Documents Relatifs a l'Histoire de Paris Pendant la Revolution Francaise... (Brookhaven) 0999-100%/U

Columbia University Oral History Collection (MCA) 1020-In Progress/O

La Condition Ouvriere en France au 19e Siecle (Hachette) 1025-100%/O

Contemporary Legal Periodical Series (Rothman) 1055-In Progress/O

The Controller's Library Collection of Her Majesty's Stationery Office Publications 1922-1977 (HDI) 1070-In Progress/O

Corporate Microfile (National Databank) 1085-In Progress(?)/O

Corpus Scriptorum Historiae Byzantiae (Microcard) 1093-100%/O

Corpus Scriptorum Ecclesiasticorum Latinorum (Microcard) 1094-100%/O

County Histories of the Old Northwest (RP) 1095-In Progress/O

County and Regional Histories (RP) 1096-100%/R

Covent Garden Prompt Books (B & H) 1097-100%/O & U

Crime and Juvenile Delinquency (MCA) 1120-100%/O, -In Progress/U

Current National Statistical Compendiums on Microfiche (CIS/Greenwood) 1140-In Progress/O

Curriculum Guides in Microfiche 1970-1980 (Kraus) 1160-In Progress(?)/O

Declassified Documents Reference System 1975- (Carrollton) 1170-In Progress/O

Dime Novels (UMI) 1180-100%/O

Disclosure (Disclosure) 1190-In Progress/O

Documents on Contemporary China 1949-1975 (Kraus/Johnson) 1200-100%/O

ERIC. Educational Resources Information Center Reports (ERIC) 3490 [For practical purposes there is no cataloging of this set; some libraries enter records for scattered titles into OCLC; one library uses index tapes in its in house system.]

Early American Imprints: First Series (Evans) 1639-1800 (Readex) 1231-In Progress/In House System [Library plans to load records into RLIN and OCLC if possible.]

Early American Imprints: Second Series (Shaw-Shoemaker) 1801-1819 (Readex) 1232-In Progress/R

Early American Newspapers 1704-1820 (Readex) 1250-In Progress/O, U, & R

Early British Periodicals (UMI) 1270-In Progress/O & R

Early English Books: Series II, 1641-1700 (Wing) [UMI is cataloging from Unit 33 onward.]

Early English Courtesy Books 1571-1773 (B & H) 1290-In Progress/O

Early English Newspapers 1662-1820 + supplements (RP) 1300-In Progress/O & R

Early English Text Society Publications. Original and Extra Series (Microcard) 1303-In Progress/O, -100%/U

Early Quaker Writings - Second Series: 17th Century (World) 1316-100%/O

Early Quaker Writings, 1650-1750 (World) 1315-100%/O

Early Rare Photographic Books. Series A: The Northwestern Museum of Science and Industry Collection (World) 1320-100%/U

Ecumenism Research Agency Publications (Ecum Res Agency) 1325-In Progress/O & R

Eighteenth-Century Sources for the Study of English Literature and Culture (Micrographics 2) 1350-In Progress/O

Energyfiche (EIC) 1360-In Progress/O

The English Gift Books and Literary Annuals 1823-1857 (Chadwyck-Healey) 1400-In Progress/O

English Literary Periodicals (UMI) 1440-In Progress/O & R

Appendix F -- Sets Cataloged on One or More Bibliographic Utilities

English and American Plays of the 19th Century: English Plays 1801-1900; American
    Plays 1831-1900 (Readex) 1370-100%/O [Set Processing]
European Official Statistical Serials on Microfiche (Chadwyck-Healey) 1460-In
    Progress/O
Federal Labor and Immigration Reports on Microfiche (Redgrave) 1477-100%/W
Federal Royal Commissions in Canada 1867-1979 (Micromedia) 1480-In Progress/U
Fin-de-Siecle Symbolist and Avant-Garde Periodicals (RP) 1500-100%/U & R
Food and Nutrition (MCA) 1525-In Progress/O
French Revolution: Critical Works and Historical Sources (General) 1600-In Progress/O
French Voyagers in the Mediterranean. 16th-18th Centuries (Hachette) 1611-100%/U
German Drama (General) 1640-In Progress/O
The Gerritsen Collection of Women's History (MCA) 1660-In Progress/O
Great Britain. House of Commons. Parliamentary Papers. 1975/76- (Chadwyck-Healey)
    1691-In Progress(?)/System designated "other"
Great Britain. Yearbook. Mayards (Trans Media) 1705-100%/O
HRAF Microfiles (Human Rel Ar F) 1860-In Progress/O & W
Hakluyt Society. Publications. Series 1-2 (Microcard) 1715-100%/U
Health, Physical Education and Recreation Microform Publications (U of Oregon)
    1740-In Progress/O
Herstory (Women's Hist RC) 1750-In Progress/O, -100%/R
Historic American Building Survey (Chadwyck-Healey) 1770-In Progress/O
History of Medicine (IDC) 1800-In Progress/O
History of Photography (RP) 1810-In Progress/U
History of Women (RP) 1830-In Progress(?)/R, Partly Cataloged/O
Holback and His Friends (Hachette) 1835
Housing and Urban Affairs 1965-1976 + supplements (MCA) 1850-In Progress/O
Indian Claims Commission Series: The Library of American Indian Affairs
    (Clearwater) 1900-In Progress/O & R
International Population Census Publications (RP) 1970-In Progress/O & R
Irish Political and Radical Newspapers of the 20th Century: Phase I, 1896-1941
    (Irish Micro) 1980-In Progress/In House System
JSAJ: Catalog of Selected Documents in Psychology (Kraus/Johnson) 2030-In Progress/O
Jeffersonian Americana (IHS) 2010-In Progress/O
The Jewish Press in the Netherlands, 1674-1950 [subset of no. 2020] (IDC) 2021-100%/R
Jewish Studies Microfiche Project (IDC) 2020-In Progress/O
Jewish Theological Seminary of America. Collections. (UMI) 2022 [The publisher has
    cataloged Adler, History of Science, and Maimonides on OCLC.]
Kentucky Culture (Lost Cause) 2040-In Progress/O
Lambeth Palace Library. [Manuscript Collections] (World) 2060-In Progress(?)/O & U
Landmarks of Science (Part I) (Readex) 2071-100%/O [Set Processing], -In Progress/R
Landmarks of Science II (Readex) 2072-100%/O [Set Processing], -In Progress/R
Latin American and Caribbean Official Statistical Serials on Microfiche (Chadwyck-
    Healey) 2080-In Progress/O
Law Books Recommended for Libraries (Rothman) 2109-In Progress(?)/O
League of Nations Documents and Serial Publications 1919-1946 (RP) 2120-In Progress/O
The Left In Britain (Harvester) 2140-In Progress(?)/O
Library of Church Unity Periodicals in Microfilm (Mf Svcs & Sales) 2185-100%/O, -In
    Progress/R(?)
The Library of Thomas Jefferson (Microcard) 2195-100%(?)/O
The Literature of Folklore (General) 2220-In Progress/O

The Literature of Theology and Church History: British Theological Studies (Lost
    Cause) 2230-In Progress/O & R
The Literature of Theology and Church History: Church History in the United
    States of America (Lost Cause) 2231-In Progress/O
Little Magazines Series 1889-1972 (World) 2240-100%/R
Mackenzie Valley Pipeline Inquiry. Briefs and Transcripts of Public Hearings
    (Micromedia) 2280-100%/System designated "other"
Manuscripta (St Louis Univ) 2295-In Progress/O & R
Medieval Manuscripts in Microform. Series I. Major Treasures in the Bodleian
    Library (Oxford Microf) 2311-In Progress/O, -In Progress(?)/R & U
Medina's Biblioteca Hispano-Americana (General) 2320-In Progress/O
Micro-Miniprints (Hein) 2327-In Progress(?)/O
Microbook Library of American Civilization (LRI) 2325-In Progress/O [Cataloging
    records are also available in tape from Western Illinois Univ.]
Microbook Library of English Literature (LRI) 2326-In Progress/O [Cataloging
    records are also available in tape from Western Illinois Univ.]
Microfiche of Books Listed in Law Books Recommended for Libraries (AALS) (Rothman)
    2331-In Progress/O, U, & W
Microlog (Micromedia) 2360-In Progress/U
Middle East Development Documents on Microfiche (IDC) 2370-In Progress(?)/O
Missionary Periodicals from the China Mainland (Greenwood/CIS) 2380-In Progress/R
Modern Indonesia Microfiche Project (IDC) 2397-In Progress/O
MusiCache (B & H) 2410-100%/System designated "other"
National Development Plans (IDC) 2430-In Progress(?)/O
The Negro: Emancipation to World War I (IHS) 2440-100%/O
New York Court of Appeals Records and Briefs, 1981- (Hein) 2466-In Progress/O
Nineteenth Century American Literature and History: Ohio Valley and the South (Lost
    Cause) 2490-In Progress/O
Nineteenth Century American Literature and History: Trans Mississippi West (Lost
    Cause) 2491-In Progress/O
Nineteenth Century Popular British Drama Acting Editions (U of Washington Pr)
    2494-100%/O
Nineteenth Century Russia: Contemporary French Opinion (Hachette) 2500-100%/O
O.S.S./State Department Intelligence and Research Reports (Univ Pub Am) 2540-In
    Progress/O & U
Pamphlets in American History (MCA) 2550 [Only the segment on women is being
    cataloged on OCLC]
Panama Canal Studies (Lib of Congress) 2549-100%/O
Pedagogic Theory in 18th Century France (Hachette) 2558-100%/U
Peel Bibliography on Microfiche (Bibliography of the Prairie Provinces to 1953)
    (Nat Lib Canada) 2560-In Progress/U(?), [Records are available in machine-
    readable form from Carleton Univ.]
Pennsylvania Side Reports 2565-In Progress/O(?), -In Progress/W
Periodicals in Musicology (Research Micro Pub) 2572-In Progress/O
Phelps-Stokes Fellowship Papers (Univ of Virginia) 2575-100%/O
Phonefiche (B & H) 2580-In Progress/O
Presidential Election Campaign Biographies 1824-1972 (UMI) 2650-100%/O
Presidential Papers Microfilms (Lib of Congress) 2652-100%/O
Profile: Canadian Provincial Government Publications on Microfiche (Micromedia)
    2660-In Progress/U
Publicat: A Canadian Federal Documents Service (Micromedia) 2680-In Progress/U

The Publications of the English Record Societies 1835-1970 (Chadwyck-Healey) 2691-
    In Progress/O
Published Colonial Records of the American Colonies (RP) 2700-100%/O, -In Progress(?)/
Quaker Women's Diaries (World) 2707-100%/O
RIDIM: Repertoire International d'Iconographie Musicale (IDC) 2870-In Progress/O, -
    100%/R
Radical Periodicals in the United States, 1880-1960 (Greenwood/CIS) 2730-100%/O & R
Radical Periodicals of Great Britain 1794-1950 (Greenwood/CIS) 2740-100%/In House
    System
Recherche en histoire sociale (Hachette) 2809-100%/U
Records of the States of the United States (Lib of Congress) 2813-In Progress/O
Records of the Church of England During the Commonwealth Period, 1653-61 (World)
    2814-100%/O
Rehabilitation and Handicapped Literature, 1950 on (MCA) 2825-In Progress/O
Revistas Hispano-Americanos (General) 2846-In Progress/O
Rhoda Kellog Child Art Collection (IHS) 2850-100%/O
The Rolls Series. (Rerum Britannicarum Medii Aevi Scriptores) (Microcard) 1703-In
    Progress/W & O(?)
Rosenbach, A.S.W. Early American Children's Books (Kraus) 2890-100%/O
Russian Historical Sources: First Series (Readex) 2991-In Progress/O
Russian Historical Sources: Second Series (Readex) 2992-In Progress/O
Russian History and Culture (UMI) 3000-In Progress/O & R
Russian Revolutionary Literature (RP) 3020-In Progress/O
Sahel: Documents and Dissertations (UMI) 3024-100%/O
Schomburg Center for Research in Black Culture: A Selection from the Schomburg
    Center: II (Kraus/3M) 3042-In Progress(?)/O
Science Fiction Periodicals Series I: 1926-1945 (Greenwood/CIS) 3051-In Progress/O
Science Fiction Periodicals Series II (Greenwood/CIS) 3052-In Progress/O
Selected Americana from Sabin's Dictionary of Books Relating to America (Lost
    Cause) 3060-In Progress/O
Session Laws of American States and Territories (Hein/UMI/IHS) 3062-In Progress/O
Slavery Source Materials (IHS) 3120-100%/O
Sexual Politics in Britain (Harvester) 3090-In Progress?/O
Slavery: Source Material and Critical Literature (Lost Cause) 3110-In Progress/O & R
Social and Economic Development Plans (See also 2430) (IDC) 3150-In Progress(?)/R
Society of Ancient French Texts. Publications (Microcard) 3165-100%/U
Sorciers, Demonologues, Magistrats, Theologiens et Medicins aus XVIe et XVIIe
    Siecles (Hachette) 3170-100%/O & U
Source Materials in the Field of Theatre (UMI) 3180-100%/O
South Asian Art (IDC) 3190-100%/O
Spanish Drama (General) 3200-In Progress/O
Stanford University Project. South Oral History Collection (MCA) 3225-100%/O
State Constitutional Conventions, Commissions, and Amendments on Microfiche
    (Greenwood/CIS) 3235-In Progress/O
State Reports on Correction and Punishment, Poverty and Public Welfare, Prior to
    1930 (Kraus/Redgrave) 3260-100%/R
Statistics Canada Publications 1851- (Micromedia) 3270-In Progress/System
    designated "other"
Tests in Microfiche (Educ Testing S) 3290-In Progress/O
Le Theatre de la Revolution et de l'Empire (Clearwater) 3300-100%/U
Theology and the History of Religion (Lost Cause) 3310-In Progress/O

Appendix F — Sets Cataloged on One or More Bibliographic Utilities

Three Centuries of English and American Plays 1500-1830 (Readex) 3320-100%/O [Set Processing]

Three Centuries of French Drama (General) 3330-In Progress/O

Tibetan Religious Works: PL480 and SFC Collections (Inst Adv St Wld Rel) 3335-In Progress/O

Travel Literature. Series I. The Americas (Louisville/Falls City) 3368-In Progress?/O

Travels in the Confederate States (Lost Cause) 3370-In Progress/O

Travels in the New South I, Thomas D. Clark (Lost Cause) 3390-In Progress/O

Travels in the New South II: Thomas D. Clark (Lost Cause) 3391-In Progress/O

Travels in the Old South I (Lost Cause) 3400-In Progress/O

Travels in the Old South II (Lost Cause) 3402-In Progress/O

Travels in the Old South III (Lost Cause) 3403-In Progress/O

Travels in the West, Southwest and Northwest (Lost Cause) 3410-In Progress/O

Trinity College, Cambridge, Library. The Mediaeval Manuscript Collection (World) 3430-In Progress/O

Underground Press Collection (B & H) 3460-In Progress/O

The Underground and Alternative Press in Britain 1961-1972; 1973- (Harvester) 3450-In Progress/O & R

United Nations Documents and Official Records from 1946 to the Present (Readex) 3470-In Progress/System designated "other"

United States Census Publications in Microform 1820-1967 (CIS/Greenwood) 3475 - Partly cataloged on OCLC

United States Congressional Hearings and Committee Prints, 1956 on (Readex) 3487-In Progress(?)/O

United States Government Bibliography Masterfile 1924-1973 (Carrollton) 3500-In Progress/R

United States Government Documents (LLMC) 3503-In Progress/W

United States Joint Publications Research Service (JPRS) Reports (Readex) 3520-In Progress/O

United States National Technical Information Service. SRIM (Selected Reports in Microfiche) (NTIS) 3530 [Cataloging for some parts is being entered in OCLC]

United States. Bureau of the Census. 1st-10th Census, 1790-1880. Population Schedules (National Archives) 3474-100%/R

United States. Joint Publications Research Service (NTIS) 3521-In Progress/O

United States. Supreme Court. Records and Briefs (BNA/IHS/UMI) 3546-In Progress/W

Unpublished Manuscripts from the Great English Collections (Harvester) 3548-In Progress/O

Urban Canada/Canada Urbain (Micromedia) 3570 [Partly cataloged on UTLAS]

Utah and the Mormons (RP) 3640%/In House System

Utopies au Siecle des Lumieres (Hachette) 3646-100%/O, -In Progress/U

Valazquez, Gonzolo. Biblioteca de obras puertorriqueno (NYPL) 3650-100%/R

Victorian Fiction (General) 3690-In Progress/O

Western Americana (UMI) 3720-100%/O

Western Americana: Frontier History of the Trans-Mississippi West 1550-1900 (RP) 3730-100%/O

William S. Gray Research Collection in Reading (A T Burrows Instit) 3750 -In Progress(?)/O

Women and Law (Women's Hist RC) 3820-In Progress/R

World Council of Churches. Faith and Order Commission. Official Pamphlets and Publications (Tex Christ Univ) 3845-100%/O

Microform Sets For Which Cataloging is Available
Wholly or Partly on One or More In-House Cataloging Systems

This list contains the titles of sets that survey respondents reported to be wholly or partly cataloged on one or more in-house cataloging systems. Like those listed in Appendix F, the sets listed here are accompanied by an abbreviated or shortened version of the publisher's name (in parentheses) together with the four-digit number used for identifying the set in the clearinghouse data base.

Agrarian Periodicals in the United States 1920-1960 (Greenwood/CIS) 0090
American Architectural Books (RP) 0120
American Culture: Series I, 1493-1806 (UMI) 0141
American Culture: Series II, 1493-1875 (UMI) 0142
American Fiction 1774-1900: Lyle H. Wright (Lost Cause) 0160
American Indian Periodicals in the Princeton University Library (Clearwater) 0200
American Natural History (RP) 0230
American Periodicals: Series I, 18th Century (UMI) 0261
American Periodicals: Series II, 1800-1850 (UMI) 0262
American Periodicals: Series III, 1850-1900 (UMI) 0263
Annual Reports of Major American Corporations (MIMC) 0358
Archives de la Linguistique Francaise: Coll de Documents Relatifs a la
    Langue Francaise 1500-1900 (France Expans) 0420
Black Journals: Phase I (Greenwood/CIS) 0543
Black Journals: Phase II (Greenwood/CIS) 0544
Books About North American Indians on Microfilm (MCA) 0560
British Periodicals in the Creative Arts (UMI) 0740
Canada Labour Papers on Microfilm in the Labour Canada Library (Pub Arc/Canada) 0815
Canadian Institute for Historical Micro-Reproduction: Microfiche Collection (CIHM) 0860
Canadian Newspapers on Microfilm (CLA) 0870
Chicago Visual Library. Text-Fiche Publications (U of Chicago Pr) 0935
Columbia University Oral History Collection (MCA) 1020
Early American Newspapers 1704-1820 (Readex) 1250
Early British Periodicals (UMI) 1270
Early English Newspapers 1662-1820 + supplements (RP) 1300
English Literary Periodicals (UMI) 1440
The Gerritsen Collection of Women's History (MCA) 1660
Health, Physical Education and Recreation Microform Publications (U of Oregon) 1740
The Rolls Series. (Rerum Britannicarum Medii Aevi Scriptores) (Microcard) 1703
Herstory (Women's Hist RC) 1750
History of Women (RP) 1830
International Population Census Publications (RP) 1970
Irish Political and Radical Newspapers of the 20th Century: Phase I, 1896-
    1941 (Irish Micro) 1980

Kentucky Culture (Lost Cause) 2040
Latin American and Caribbean Official Statistical Serials on Microfiche
   (Chadwyck-Healey) 2080
The Left In Britain (Harvester) 2140
Library of Church Unity Periodicals in Microfilm (Mf Svcs & Sales) 2185
The Literature of Folklore (General) 2220
Microbook Library of American Civilization (LRI) 2325
Microbook Library of English Literature (LRI) 2326
Nineteenth Century American Literature and History: Ohio Valley and the
   South (Lost Cause) 2490
Peel Bibliography on Microfiche (Bibliography of the Prairie Provinces to
   1953) (Nat Lib Canada) 2560
The Plains and the Rockies (Lost Cause) 2600
Published Colonial Records of the American Colonies (RP) 2700
Radical Periodicals of Great Britain 1794-1950 (Greenwood/CIS) 2740
Russian Historical Sources: First Series (Readex) 2991
Russian Historical Sources: Second Series (Readex) 2992
Slavery Source Materials (IHS) 3120
Social and Economic Development Plans (See also 2430) (IDC) 3150
State Reports on Correction and Punishment, Poverty and Public Welfare,
   Prior to 1930 (Kraus/Redgrave) 3260
Underground Press Collection (B & H) 3460
The Underground and Alternative Press in Britain 1961-1972; 1973-
   (Harvester) 3450
United States National Technical Information Service. SRIM (Selected Reports
   in Microfiche) (NTIS) 3530
Urban Canada/Canada Urbain (Micromedia) 3570
Utah and the Mormons (RP) 3640
Western Americana: Frontier History of the Trans-Mississippi West 1550-1900 (RP) 3730
Women and Law (Women's Hist RC) 3820

Appendix H

85 Microform Sets Given Highest Priority for Cataloging in the Microform Project Survey - Listed in Alphabetical Order

American Architectural Books (RP) - 0120
American Culture: Series I, 1493-1806 (UMI) - 0141
American Culture: Series II, 1493-1875 (UMI) - 0142
American Fiction 1774-1900 (RP) - 0151
American Fiction 1901-1910 (RP) - 0152
American Fiction 1774-1900: Lyle H. Wright (Lost Cause) - 0160
American Periodicals: Series I, 18th Century (UMI) - 0261
American Periodicals: Series II, 1800-1850 (UMI) - 0262
American Periodicals: Series III, 1850-1900 (UMI) - 0263
Anti-Slavery Propaganda in the Oberlin College Library (Lost Cause) - 0380
Art Exhibition Catalogues on Microfiche (Chadwyck-Healey) - 0470
ASI Microfiche Library (American Statistics Index). (CIS) - 0500
Black Culture Collection (B & H) - 0540
British and Continental Rhetoric and Elocution (UMI) - 0610
CIS Microfiche Library. (CIS) - 0970
CIS U.S. Serial Set on Microfiche (CIS) - 0980
City Directories of the United States (RP) - 0990
College Catalog Collection, Microfiche (Nat Micro Lib) - 1000
Columbia University Oral History Collection (MCA) - 1020
Confederate Imprints. (RP) - 1040
Crime and Juvenile Delinquency (MCA) - 1120
Curriculum Development Library (Fearon Pitman) - 1150
Early American Imprints: First Series (Evans) 1639-1800 (Readex) - 1231
Early American Imprints: Second Series (Shaw-Shoemaker) 1801-1819 (Readex) - 1232
Early American Newspapers 1704-1820 (Readex) - 1250
Early British Periodicals (UMI) - 1270
Early English Books: Series I, 1475-1640 (Pollard and Redgrave) (UMI) - 1281
Early English Books: Series II, 1641-1700 (Wing) (UMI) - 1282
Early English Newspapers 1662-1820 + supplements (RP) - 1300
Early English Text Society Publications. Original and Extra Series.
    (Microcard) - 1303
Ecumenism Research Agency Publications. (Ecum Res Agency) - 1325
Eighteenth Century Sources for the Study of English Literature and Culture
    (Micrographics 2) - 1350
English and American Plays of the 19th Century: English Plays 1801-1900;
    American Plays 1831-1900 (Readex) - 1370
English Literary Periodicals (UMI) - 1440
Fowler Collection of Early Architectural Books (RP) - 1530
French Books before 1601 (General) - 1540
French Political Pamphlets from 1560 to 1653. (B & H) - 1590
German Baroque Literature: Harold Jantz Collection (RP) - 1621
German Baroque Literature: Yale Collection (RP) - 1622
German Books before 1601 (General) - 1630
Gerritsen Collection of Women's History (MCA) - 1660
Goldsmiths'-Kress Library of Economic Literature. Segment I: Printed Books
    Through 1800 (RP) - 1670
Goldsmiths'-Kress Library of Economic Literature. Segment II: 1801-1850. (RP) - 1671
Great Britain. Parliament. Hansard's Parliamentary Debates, Lords and Commons,
    1066-on. (Readex) - 1694

Great Britain. Parliament. House of Commons. Sessional Papers. 1731-on.
    (Readex) - 1696
Health, Physical Education and Recreation Microform Publications (U of Oregon)
    - 1740
Herstory (Women's Hist RC) - 1750
History of Photography (RP) - 1810
History of Women (RP) - 1830
Housing and Urban Affairs 1965-1976 + supplements (MCA) - 1850
HRAF Microfiles (Human Rel Ar F) - 1860
International Population Census Publications (RP) - 1970
Italian Books before 1601 (General) - 1991
JSAJ: Catalog of Selected Documents in Psychology (Kraus/Johnson) - 2030
Landmarks of Science (Part I) (Readex) - 2071
Landmarks of Science II (Readex) - 2072
Manuscripta (St Louis Univ) - 2295
Microbook Library of American Civilization (LRI) - 2325
Microbook Library of English Literature (LRI) - 2326
Microfiche of Books Listed in LAW BOOKS RECOMMENDED FOR LIBRARIES (AALS).
    (Rothman) - 2331
O.S.S./State Department Intelligence and Research Reports. (Univ Pub Am) - 2540
Pamphlets in American History (MCA) - 2550
Peel Bibliography on Microfiche (Bibliography of the Prairie Provinces to
    1953) (Nat Lib Canada) - 2560
Plains and the Rockies (Lost Cause) - 2600
Rehabilitation and Handicapped Literature, 1950 on (MCA) - 2825
Russian Historical Sources: First Series. (Readex) - 2991
Russian Historical Sources: Second Series (Readex) - 2992
Schomburg Center for Research in Black Culture: A Selection from the Schomburg
    Center: I (Kraus) - 3040
Selected Americana from Sabin's DICTIONARY OF BOOKS RELATING TO AMERICA. (Lost
    Cause) - 3060
Source Materials in the Field of Theatre (UMI) - 3180
Spanish Drama of the Golden Age: The Comedia Collection of the U of
    Pennsylvania Libraries (RP) - 3210
State Censuses. (Kraus) - 3230
State Constitutional Conventions, Commissions, and Amendments on Microfiche.
    (Greenwood/CIS) - 3235
Tests in Microfiche (Educ Testing Serv) - 3290
Thomason Tracts: The Pamphlets, Books, Newspapers, and MSS Collected by Geo
    Thomason, 1640-1661 (UMI) - 3315
Three Centuries of English and American Plays 1500-1830 (Readex) - 3320
Three Centuries of French Drama (General) - 3330
Underground Press Collection. (B & H) - 3460
ERIC. Educational Resources Information Center Reports. (ERIC) - 3490
United States National Technical Information Service. SRIM (Selected Reports
    in Microfiche) (NTIS) - 3530
United States Serial Set (1817 - Present) and American State Papers (1789-
    1838). (Readex) - 3545
William S. Gray Research Collection in Reading (A.T. Burrows Instit.) - 3750
Women and Health/Mental Health (Women's Hist RC) - 3810
Women and Law (Women's Hist RC) - 3820
World Council of Churches. Faith and Order Commission. Official Pamphlets and
    Publications. (Texas Christian Univ) - 3845

Appendix I

85 Microform Sets Given Highest Priority for Cataloging in the Microform Project Survey - Listed in Priority Order

1   Early American Imprints: First Series (Evans) 1639-1800 (Readex) - 1231
2   Early English Books: Series II, 1641-1700 (Wing) (UMI) - 1282
3   Early American Imprints: Second Series (Shaw-Shoemaker) 1801-1819 (Readex) - 1232
4   Early English Books: Series I, 1475-1640 (Pollard and Redgrave) (UMI) - 1281
5   Three Centuries of English and American Plays 1500-1830 (Readex) - 3320
6   American Periodicals: Series II, 1800-1850 (UMI) - 0262
7   English and American Plays of the 19th Century: English Plays 1801-1900; American Plays 1831-1900 (Readex) - 1370
8   American Periodicals: Series I, 18th Century (UMI) - 0261
9   Landmarks of Science (Part I) (Readex) - 2071
10 American Fiction 1774-1900 (RP) - 0151
11 American Periodicals: Series III, 1850-1900 (UMI) - 0263
12 HRAF Microfiles (Human Rel Ar F) - 1860
13 Herstory (Women's Hist RC) - 1750
14 Health, Physical Education and Recreation Microform Publications (U of Oregon) - 1740
15 History of Women (RP) - 1830
16 Microbook Library of English Literature (LRI) - 2326
17 American Fiction 1901-1910 (RP) - 0152
18 Microbook Library of American Civilization (LRI) - 2325
19 ERIC. Educational Resources Information Center Reports. (ERIC) - 3490
20 Women and Law (Women's Hist RC) - 3820
21 American Culture: Series II, 1493-1875 (UMI) - 0142
22 American Fiction 1774-1900: Lyle H. Wright (Lost Cause) - 0160
23 English Literary Periodicals (UMI) - 1440
24 Gerritsen Collection of Women's History (MCA) - 1660
25 Crime and Juvenile Delinquency (MCA) - 1120
26 Landmarks of Science II (Readex) - 2072
27 American Culture: Series I, 1493-1806 (UMI) - 0141
28 Spanish Drama of the Golden Age: The Comedia Collection of the U of Pennsylvania Libraries (RP) - 3210
29 Pamphlets in American History (MCA) - 2550
30 Columbia University Oral History Collection (MCA) - 1020
31 Art Exhibition Catalogues on Microfiche (Chadwyck-Healey) - 0470
32 Early English Newspapers 1662-1820 + supplements (RP) - 1300
33 College Catalog Collection, Microfiche (Nat Micro Lib) - 1000
34 Manuscripta (St Louis Univ) - 2295
35 Underground Press Collection. (B & H) - 3460
36 Thomason Tracts: The Pamphlets, Books, Newspapers, and MSS Collected by George Thomason, 1640-1661 (UMI) - 3315
37 German Baroque Literature: Yale Collection (RP) - 1622
38 Early British Periodicals (UMI) - 1270
39 Early American Newspapers 1704-1820 (Readex) - 1250
40 Women and Health/Mental Health (Women's Hist RC) - 3810
41 Housing and Urban Affairs 1965-1976 + supplements (MCA) - 1850
42 Eighteenth Century Sources for the Study of English Literature and Culture (Micrographics 2) - 1350
43 United States National Technical Information Service. SRIM (Selected Reports in Microfiche) (NTIS) - 3530

44 Goldsmiths'-Kress Library of Economic Literature. Segment I: Printed Books Through 1800 (RP) – 1670
45 Black Culture Collection (B & H) – 0540
46 Italian Books before 1601 (General) – 1991
47 German Books before 1601 (General) – 1630
48 Peel Bibliography on Microfiche (Bibliography of the Prairie Provinces to 1953) (Nat Lib Canada) – 2560
49 Russian Historical Sources: First Series. (Readex) – 2991
50 British and Continental Rhetoric and Elocution (UMI) – 0610
51 Source Materials in the Field of Theatre (UMI) – 3180
52 Plains and the Rockies (Lost Cause) – 2600
53 History of Photography (RP) – 1810
54 French Books before 1601 (General) – 1540
55 American Architectural Books (RP) – 0120
56 Anti-Slavery Propaganda in the Oberlin College Library (Lost Cause) – 0380
57 Goldsmiths'-Kress Library of Economic Literature. Segment II: 1801-1850. (RP) – 1671
58 Schomburg Center for Research in Black Culture: A Selection from the Schomburg Center: I (Kraus) – 3040
59 Selected Americana from Sabin's DICTIONARY OF BOOKS RELATING TO AMERICA. (Lost Cause) – 3060
60 World Council of Churches. Faith and Order Commission. Official Pamphlets and Publications. (Texas Christian Univ) – 3845
61 Confederate Imprints. (RP) – 1040
62 Curriculum Development Library (Fearon Pitman) – 1150
63 Microfiche of Books Listed in LAW BOOKS RECOMMENDED FOR LIBRARIES (AALS). (Rothman) – 2331
64 Rehabilitation and Handicapped Literature, 1950 on (MCA) – 2825
65 United States Serial Set (1817 – Present) and American State Papers (1789-1838). (Readex) – 3545
66 ASI Microfiche Library (American Statistics Index). (CIS) – 0500
67 International Population Census Publications (RP) – 1970
68 Three Centuries of French Drama (General) – 3330
69 City Directories of the United States (RP) – 0990
70 Great Britain. Parliament. Hansard's Parliamentary Debates, Lords and Commons, 1066-on. (Readex) – 1694
71 JSAJ: Catalog of Selected Documents in Psychology (Kraus/Johnson) – 2030
72 CIS Microfiche Library. (CIS) – 0970
73 CIS U.S. Serial Set on Microfiche (CIS) – 0980
74 Ecumenism Research Agency Publications. (Ecum Res Agency) – 1325
75 Fowler Collection of Early Architectural Books (RP) – 1530
76 German Baroque Literature: Harold Jantz Collection (RP) – 1621
77 State Constitutional Conventions, Commissions, and Amendments on Microfiche. (Greenwood/CIS) – 3235
78 Tests in Microfiche (Educ Testing Serv) – 3290
79 State Censuses. (Kraus) – 3230
80 O.S.S./State Department Intelligence and Research Reports. (Univ Pub Am) – 2540
81 Great Britain. Parliament. House of Commons. Sessional Papers. 1731-on. (Readex) – 1696
82 Early English Text Society Publications. Original and Extra Series. (Microcard) – 1303
83 French Political Pamphlets from 1560 to 1653. (B & H) – 1590
84 Russian Historical Sources: Second Series (Readex) – 2992
85 William S. Gray Research Collection in Reading (A.T. Burrows Instit.) – 3750

**Highly-Ranked Sets For Which Machine-Readable
Cataloging Is Unavailable or Very Incomplete on OCLC**

Data from Microform Project survey returns shows that, of the 85 sets that were given highest priority for cataloging, 50% have either been fully cataloged or are in the process of being cataloged on OCLC. The 43 remaining sets are listed below. The list includes all sets for which no machine-readable cataloging is shown to have been input to OCLC, along with sets for which little OCLC cataloging is shown and sets for which data is not given on the amount of OCLC cataloging that has been created. It is annotated to show where machine-readable records have been created on data bases other than OCLC.

The list is in alphabetical order by title. As is the case with other alphabetical lists in this report, capital letters appear before lower-case ones (thus ASI appears before American Fiction). The titles used are ones supplied by publishers. See the second edition of Suzanne Dodson's Microform Research Collections: a Guide (Meckler Publishing Westport, CT, 1983) for alternate titles and information regarding dates of publication and set contents. An abbreviation of publisher name follows each set title; the four-digit code which identifies the set follows that.

Note that some entries on the list are already fully indexed by the publisher (e.g. ERIC, the CIS and ASI Microfiche Libraries and the CIS U.S. Serial Set). The priority given the cataloging of these sets suggests an indexing function for cataloging that deserves further examination, though it is outside the scope of this report. Other entries are works in series rather than collections of books and serials (e.g. Hansard's Parliamentary Debates and the House of Commons Sessional Papers). The priority given the cataloging of these series may indicate a perception that they require detailed analyzing.

Significantly, as a whole, indexed sets and series entries rank rather low in the listing. The CIS Microfiche Library ranks 72nd out of 85, ASI 66th. Readex's Serial Set collection ranks 65th, while that of CIS ranks 73rd. Hansard's and the Commons Sessional Papers rank 70th and 81st respectively. ERIC is an exception: this heavily-used set was given high priority for cataloging. It ranks 19 in the list of 85.

Highly-Ranked Sets For Which Machine-Readable
Cataloging Is Unavailable or Very Incomplete on OCLC

ASI Microfiche Library (American Statistics Index/Microfiche Library)
    (CIS) - 0500
    Two libraries are cataloging in machine-readable form; one on
    an in-house system, the other on a system denoted as "other".

American Fiction 1774-1900: Lyle H. Wright (Lost Cause) 0160
  Three libraries report the production of small numbers of records on
  OCLC, in one case, cataloging is reporting as continuing, but the
  report may be in error. Two libraries report creating records on in-
  house systems.
Anti-Slavery Propaganda in the Oberlin College Library (Lost Cause) - 0380
  Three libraries report that they have produced machine-readable
  cataloging on in-house data bases. One library is shown to have
  produced OCLC cataloging, but the amount is not shown.
Black Culture Collection (B & H) - 0540
  One library reports creating records on OCLC, but the report may be in
  error.
British and Continental Rhetoric and Elocution (UMI) - 0610
  One library reports creating records on OCLC, but the report may be in
  error.
CIS Microfiche Library (CIS) - 0970
  Three libraries report the cataloging of small segments of this
  collection on OCLC.
CIS U.S. Serial Set on Microfiche (CIS) - 0980
  No machine-readable records were reported for this set.
City Directories of the United States (RP) - 0990
  One library has cataloged 1% on an in-house system. Two
  libraries have created undetermined amounts of machine-readable
  records; one on an unknown data base, the other on OCLC.
College Catalog Collection, Microfiche (Nat Micro Lib) - 1000
  There are no reports of machine-readable cataloging for this set.
Confederate Imprints (RP) - 1040
  No machine-readable records were reported for this set.
Curriculum Development Library (Fearon Pitman) - 1150
  There are no reports of machine-readable cataloging for this set.
ERIC. Educational Resource Information Center Reports (ERIC) - 3490
  There is one report of entry of a small number of records for this set
  into OCLC.
Early American Imprints: First Series (Evans) 1639-1800 (Readex) - 1231
  One library has cataloged an undetermined amount on RLIN. In
  addition, it should be noted that the American Antiquarian
  Society North American Imprints Project is cataloging the
  titles which are included in this set. Microprint card numbers
  are being included in cataloging records. AAS is creating the
  records on an in-house system, but will enter all of them into
  RLIN and is willing to have them tape-loaded into OCLC if funds
  to reimburse costs are obtained. [For greatest usefulness the
  records should be upgraded to include proper 007 and 533 notes
  and should be tagged for set processing before being loaded
  into OCLC.]
Early American Imprints: Second Series (Shaw-Shoemaker) 1801-1819 (Readex)
  - 1232
  There are no reports of OCLC cataloging for this set.

Early English Books: Series I, 1475-1640 (Pollard and Redgrave)
(UMI) - 1281
Three libraries have produced machine-readable records; one has
input 20% into RLIN, one has input an indeterminate amount into
an in-house system, and one has input an indeterminate amount
into OCLC.
Early English Books: Series II, 1641-1700 (Wing) (UMI) - 1282
One library has input records for an indeterminate percentage
of the set into OCLC.
Early English Text Society Publications. Original and Extra Series
(Microcard) - 1303
One library has cataloged this set on UTLAS; another has
produced a small quantity of OCLC records.
The Fowler Collection of Early Architectural Books (RP) - 1530
No machine-readable records were reported for this set.
French Books before 1601 (General) - 1540
No machine-readable records were reported for this set.
French Political Pamphlets from 1560 to 1653 (B & H) - 1590
No machine-readable records were reported for this set.
German Baroque Literature: Harold Jantz Collection (RP) - 1621
No machine-readable records were reported for this set.
German Baroque Literature: Yale Collection (RP) - 1622
No machine-readable records were reported for this set.
German Books before 1601 (General) - 1630
No machine-readable records were reported for this set.
Goldsmiths'-Kress Library of Economic Literature. Segment I: Printed Books
Through 1800 (RP) - 1670
Goldsmiths'-Kress Library of Economic Literature. Segment II: 1801-1850
(RP) - 1671
No machine-readable records were reported for either of these
sets. Note: there is a third part to the set which did not
meet criteria for inclusion in the list of highest-priority
sets.
Great Britain. Parliament. Hansard's Parliamentary Debates, Lords and
Commons, 1066 to present (Readex) - 1694
No machine-readable records were reported for this set.
Great Britain. Parliament. House of Commons. Sessional Papers. 1731 to
present (Readex) - 1696
No machine-readable records were reported for this set.
History of Photography (RP) - 1810
Four libraries have created machine-readable records; two on
UTLAS, one on RLIN, and one (an indeterminate amount) on OCLC.
History of Women (RP) - 1830
Five libraries have created machine-readable records; two on
in-house systems, one on RLIN, and two have create
indeterminate amounts of records both in-house and on OCLC.
Italian Books before 1601 (General) - 1991
No machine-readable records were reported for this set.
Pamphlets in American History (MCA) - 2550
There is one report of OCLC cataloging for this set: records for the
portion covering the section on women have been entered into that data
base.

Peel Bibliography on Microfiche (Bibliography of the Prairie Provinces to
 1953) (Nat Lib Canada) - 2560
  This set contains items cited in the bibliography and is not itself a
  bibliography. One library has created brief records for the entire set
  on an in-house system and two libraries have created indeterminate
  amounts of records; one on UTLAS and the other one on an in-house
  system.
The Plains and the Rockies (Lost Cause) - 2600
  Three libraries have produced machine-readable records; one has
  produced an indeterminate amount of cataloging on OCLC, one a
  small amount on an unspecified system, and one a small amount
  on an in-house system.
Russian Historical Sources: First Series (Readex) - 2991
  One library has cataloged an indeterminate amount on OCLC.
Russian Historical Sources: Second Series (Readex) - 2992
  Five libraries have produced machine-readable cataloging; two
  of them indeterminate amounts in-house, one of them an
  indeterminate amount on an unspecified system, and one an
  indeterminate amount on OCLC.
Schomburg Center for Research in Black Culture: A Selection from the
 Schomburg Center: I (Kraus) - 3040
  One library has produced a small amount of machine-readable
  cataloging on an unspecified system.
Spanish Drama of the Golden Age: The Comedia Collection of the U of
 Pennsylvania Libraries (RP) - 3210
  One library has cataloged about half this set on OCLC, but
  cataloging is not shown to be continuing.
State Censuses (Kraus) - 3230
  One library has cataloged an indeterminate amount on OCLC.
The Thomason Tracts: The Pamphlets, Books, Newspapers, and MSS Collected by
 George Thomason, 1640-1661 (UMI) - 3315
  No machine-readable records were reported for this set.
United States Serial Set (1817 to Present) and American State Papers (1789-
 1838) (Readex) - 3545
  One library has cataloged approximately 60% of this set on a
  system denoted "other".
William S. Gray Research Collection in Reading (A T Burrows Ins) - 3750
  Three libraries have created OCLC records, two have cataloged
  indeterminate amounts and one reports cataloging 70% but gives
  little other data.
Women and Health/Mental Health (Women's Hist RC) - 3810
  No machine-readable records were reported for this set.
Women and Law (Women's Hist RC) - 3820
  No machine-readable records were reported for this set.

Appendix K

Highly-Ranked Sets For Which Machine-Readable Cataloging
is Unavailable or Very Imcomplete on RLIN

This listing was created in the same manner as Appendix J. For further information, see the introduction to that appendix. Where no comment is given, no cataloging was reported for the set.

American Architectural Books (RP) - 0120
American Culture: Series I, 1493-1806 (UMI) - 0141
American Culture: Series II, 1493-1875 (UMI) - 0142
American Fiction 1774-1900 (RP) - 0151
    Yale has cataloged a small portion of this set, partly on RLIN and partly on OCLC.
American Fiction 1901-1910 (RP) - 0152
American Fiction 1774-1900: Lyle H. Wright (Lost Cause) - 0160
Anti-Slavery Propaganda in the Oberlin College Library (Lost Cause) - 0380
Art Exhibition Catalogues on Microfiche (Chadwyck-Healey) - 0470
ASI Microfiche Library (American Statistics Index/Microfiche Library) (CIS) - 0500
Black Culture Collection (B & H) - 0540
British and Continental Rhetoric and Elocution (UMI) - 0610
CIS Microfiche Library (CIS) - 0970
CIS U.S. Serial Set on Microfiche (CIS) - 0980
City Directories of the United States (RP) - 0990
Columbia University Oral History Collection (MCA) - 1020
Confederate Imprints (RP) - 1040
Crime and Juvenile Delinquency (MCA) - 1120
ERIC. Educational Resources Information Center Reports (ERIC) - 3490
Early American Imprints: First Series (Evans) 1639-1800 (Readex) - 1231
Early English Books: Series I, 1475-1640 (Pollard and Redgrave) (UMI) - 1281
    The New York Public Library has created RLIN records for this set since 1973.
Early English Books: Series II, 1641-1700 (Wing) (UMI) - 1282
Early English Text Society Publications. Original and Extra Series (Microcard) - 1303
Eighteenth-Century Sources for the Study of English Literature and Culture (Micrographics 2) - 1350
English and American Plays of the 19th Century: English Plays 1801-1900; American Plays 1831-1900 (Readex) - 1370
The Fowler Collection of Early Architectural Books (RP) - 1530
French Books before 1601 (General) - 1540
French Political Pamphlets from 1560 to 1653 (B & H) - 1590
German Baroque Literature: Harold Jantz Collection (RP) - 1621
German Baroque Literature: Yale Collection (RP) - 1622
German Books before 1601 (General) - 1630
The Gerritsen Collection of Women's History (MCA) - 1660
Goldsmiths'-Kress Library of Economic Literature. Segment I: Printed Books Through 1800 (RP) - 1670
Goldsmiths'-Kress Library of Economic Literature. Segment II: 1801-1850 (RP) - 1671
Great Britain. Parliament. Hansard's Parliamentary Debates, Lords and Commons, 1066 on (Readex) - 1694

Great Britain. Parliament. House of Commons. Sessional Papers. 1731-on (Readex) - 1696

Health, Physical Education and Recreation Microform Publications (U of Oregon) - 1740
    The University of California at Davis has cataloged part of this set; the
    response does not make it clear whether the cataloging is in machine-
    readable form.

History of Photography (RP) - 1810

Housing and Urban Affairs 1965-1976 + supplements (MCA) - 1850

HRAF Microfiles (Human Rel Ar F) - 1860

Italian Books before 1601 (General) - 1991

JSAJ: Catalog of Selected Documents in Psychology (Kraus/Johnson) - 2030

Landmarks of Science (Part I) (Readex) - 2071

Landmarks of Science II (Readex) - 2072
    The New York Public Library is shown to have created machine-readable
    records for 5% of the two Landmarks sets.

Microbook Library of American Civilization (LRI) - 2325

Microbook Library of English Literature (LRI) - 2326

Microfiche of Books Listed in Law Books Recommended for Libraries (AALS)
    (Rothman) - 2331

O.S.S./State Department Intelligence and Research Reports (Univ Pub Am) - 2540

Pamphlets in American History (MCA) - 2550

Peel Bibliography on Microfiche (Bibliography of the Prairie Provinces to 1953)
    (Nat Lib Canada) - 2560

The Plains and the Rockies (Lost Cause) - 2600

Rehabilitation and Handicapped Literature, 1950 on (MCA) - 2825

Russian Historical Sources: First Series (Readex) - 2991

Russian Historical Sources: Second Series (Readex) - 2992

Schomburg Center for Research in Black Culture: A Selection from the Schomburg
    Center: I (Kraus) - 3040

Selected Americana from Sabin's Dictionary of Books Relating to America (Lost
    Cause) - 3060

Source Materials in the Field of Theatre (UMI) - 3180

Spanish Drama of the Golden Age: The Comedia Collection of the U of Pennsylvania
    Libraries (RP) - 3210

State Censuses (Kraus) - 3230

State Constitutional Conventions, Commissions, and Amendments on Microfiche
    (Greenwood/CIS) - 3235

The Thomason Tracts: The Pamphlets, Books, Newspapers, and MSS Collected by Geo
    Thomason, 1640-1661 (UMI) - 3315

Three Centuries of English and American Plays 1500-1830 (Readex) - 3320

Three Centuries of French Drama (General) - 3330

Underground Press Collection (B & H) - 3460

United States National Technical Information Service. SRIM (Selected Reports in
    Microfiche) (NTIS) - 3530

United States Serial Set (1817 to Present) and American State Papers (1789-1838)
    (Readex) - 3545

William S. Gray Research Collection in Reading (A T Burrows Ins) - 3750

Women and Health/Mental Health (Women's Hist RC) - 3810

Women and Law (Women's Hist RC) - 3820
    The Los Angeles County Public Library has created some records for this
    set both on RLIN and an in-house system.

World Council of Churches. Faith and Order Commission. Official Pamphlets
    and Publications (Tex Christ Univ) - 3845

Appendix L

Highly-Ranked Sets For Which Machine-Readable Cataloging
is Unavailable or Very Imcomplete on UTLAS

This listing was created in the same manner as Appendix J. For
further information, see the introduction to that appendix. No cataloging
was reported for any of the sets listed here.

American Architectural Books (RP) - 0120
American Culture: Series I, 1493-1806 (UMI) - 0141
American Culture: Series II, 1493-1875 (UMI) - 0142
American Fiction 1774-1900 (RP) - 0151
American Fiction 1901-1910 (RP) - 0152
American Fiction 1774-1900: Lyle H. Wright (Lost Cause) - 0160
American Periodicals: Series I, 18th Century (UMI) - 0261
American Periodicals: Series II, 1800-1850 (UMI) - 0262
American Periodicals: Series III, 1850-1900 (UMI) - 0263
Anti-Slavery Propaganda in the Oberlin College Library (Lost Cause) - 0380
ASI Microfiche Library (American Statistics Index/Microfiche Library) (CIS) - 0500
Black Culture Collection (B & H) - 0540
British and Continental Rhetoric and Elocution (UMI) - 0610
CIS Microfiche Library (CIS) - 0970
CIS U.S. Serial Set on Microfiche (CIS) - 0980
City Directories of the United States (RP) - 0990
College Catalog Collection, Microfiche (Nat Micro Lib) - 1000
Columbia University Oral History Collection (MCA) - 1020
Confederate Imprints (RP) - 1040
Curriculum Development Library (Fearon Pitman) - 1150
ERIC. Educational Resources Information Center Reports (ERIC) - 3490
Early American Imprints: First Series (Evans) 1639-1800 (Readex) - 1231
Early American Imprints: Second Series (Shaw-Shoemaker) 1801-1819 (Readex) - 1232
Early British Periodicals (UMI) - 1270
Early English Books: Series I, 1475-1640 (Pollard and Redgrave) (UMI) - 1281
Early English Books: Series II, 1641-1700 (Wing) (UMI) - 1282
Early English Newspapers 1662-1820 + supplements (RP) - 1300
Ecumenism Research Agency Publications (Ecum Res Agency) - 1325
Eighteenth-Century Sources for the Study of English Literature and Culture
    (Micrographics 2) - 1350
English and American Plays of the 19th Century: English Plays 1801-1900; American
    Plays 1831-1900 (Readex) - 1370
English Literary Periodicals (UMI) - 1440
The Fowler Collection of Early Architectural Books (RP) - 1530
French Books before 1601 (General) - 1540
French Political Pamphlets from 1560 to 1653 (B & H) - 1590
German Baroque Literature: Harold Jantz Collection (RP) - 1621
German Baroque Literature: Yale Collection (RP) - 1622
German Books before 1601 (General) - 1630

The Gerritsen Collection of Women's History (MCA) - 1660
Goldsmiths'-Kress Library of Economic Literature. Segment I: Printed Books Through 1800 (RP) - 1670
Goldsmiths'-Kress Library of Economic Literature. Segment II: 1801-1850 (RP) - 1671
Great Britain. Parliament. Hansard's Parliamentary Debates, Lords and Commons, 1066 on (Readex) - 1694
Great Britain. Parliament. House of Commons. Sessional Papers. 1731-on (Readex) - 1696
Herstory (Women's Hist RC) - 1750
History of Women (RP) - 1830
Housing and Urban Affairs 1965-1976 + supplements (MCA) - 1850
HRAF Microfiles (Human Rel Ar F) - 1860
International Population Census Publications (RP) - 1970
Italian Books before 1601 (General) - 1991
JSAJ: Catalog of Selected Documents in Psychology (Kraus/Johnson) - 2030
Landmarks of Science (Part I) (Readex) - 2071
Landmarks of Science II (Readex) - 2072
Manuscripta (St Louis Univ) - 2295
Microbook Library of American Civilization (LRI) - 2325
Microbook Library of English Literature (LRI) - 2326
Pamphlets in American History (MCA) - 2550
Peel Bibliography on Microfiche (Bibliography of the Prairie Provinces to 1953) (Nat Lib Canada) - 2560
The Plains and the Rockies (Lost Cause) - 2600
Rehabilitation and Handicapped Literature, 1950 on (MCA) - 2825
Russian Historical Sources: First Series (Readex) - 2991
Russian Historical Sources: Second Series (Readex) - 2992
Schomburg Center for Research in Black Culture: A Selection from the Schomburg Center: I (Kraus) - 3040
Selected Americana from Sabin's Dictionary of Books Relating to America (Lost Cause) - 3060
Source Materials in the Field of Theatre (UMI) - 3180
Spanish Drama of the Golden Age: The Comedia Collection of the U of Pennsylvania Libraries (RP) - 3210
State Censuses (Kraus) - 3230
State Constitutional Conventions, Commissions, and Amendments on Microfiche (Greenwood/CIS) - 3235
Tests in Microfiche (Educ Testing S) - 3290
The Thomason Tracts: The Pamphlets, Books, Newspapers, and MSS Collected by Geo Thomason, 1640-1661 (UMI) - 3315
Three Centuries of English and American Plays 1500-1830 (Readex) - 3320
Three Centuries of French Drama (General) - 3330
Underground Press Collection (B & H) - 3460
United States Serial Set (1817 to Present) and American State Papers (1789-1838) (Readex) -
William S. Gray Research Collection in Reading (A T Burrows Ins) - 3750
Women and Health/Mental Health (Women's Hist RC) - 3810
Women and Law (Women's Hist RC) - 3820
World Council of Churches. Faith and Order Commission. Official Pamphlets and Publications (Tex Christ Univ) - 3845

Sample Comments Given on or with Survey Returns

This appendix contains a sampling of general statements made both in letters and as comments in connection with the Microform Project Survey. The collection includes both typical and unusual comments, and, as a whole, is not meant to be representative of all comments received.

Our first efforts at surveying our holdings were so discouraging that we decided not to respond at all. Looking at your follow-up letter, I thought I would at least send along the results of our census together with as much information about cataloging as I could easily gather.

Just finding out what we have has taken a paraprofessional three days and even so this is certainly not a complete list. We treat most microform sets as publishers' series; when we catalog the titles separately we do not make an added entry for the title of the set. Fortunately some of my colleagues have long memories or their own systems of record keeping.

Despite some misgivings about the questionnaire, there was a good deal of interest here in the project and I would certainly like to be placed on the project mailing list. Because of a large monograph backlog and a retrospective conversion project, I doubt that we will be in a position to participate in any shared cataloging project at any time in the next year or two, but I certainly hope that will not be the case for too long.

Frankly, we found the questionnaire more in the nature of a research project that a survey. To answer many of the items on the response form would have required considerable digging for information.

Many of the purchases were made years ago and there is no record of whether we purchased the entire set or if the definition of an entire set is changed over the years.

I did not return Part III of the questionnaire. We could not establish priorities for the various titles. Philosophically I remain committed to cooperative cataloging for microforms. For several years I endeavored to interest the state universities in [state] to embark on such a project. There was little interest. Now the cost of such a project in FTU and catalog card/tape record changes make such a project unachievable. The thrust of libraries' efforts should be directed to the producers of microforms to encourage them to make available quality machine readable cataloging.

The survey sheets which we received have led to discussion on the future of microforms at [library] which has been instructive and welcome.

The exercise of completing the questionnaire was helpful to me in reviewing our cataloging policies and the state of bibliographical control of our holdings in microform.

Our director is well aware that this [i.e. microform cataloging] should be an area of greater concern. We have much room for improvement in our handling of non-print collections. In fact, the director is using the survey to initiate discussions with various groups and committees within the library on establishing reasonable policies and procedures for non-print materials.

I want to affirm our interest and willingness to be involved in future developments but would find it impossible to participate while our staffing shrinks over the next three years.

Since we fully recognize the importance of the survey, I am most reluctant to say outright that we cannot manage Part II, but we are very short in staff in this area ....

I have no doubts that even with all the time I spent ferreting out these titles there are still more remaining in hiding under who-knows-what headings! Although I have grumbled a lot while working on the survey it certainly has been a wonderful tool in acquainting me with our collection.

We are both interested and committed to working with a cooperative microform cataloging project using the OCLC data base.

Thank you for the opportunity to participate in this project; the process was very useful to us.

It is an interesting project and it is gratifying to see some positive efforts toward resource and information sharing. We would very much appreciate receiving copies of the summary reports which we could use in our instructional program.

We look forward to the project report, hoping that it and the interest and effort which may be garnered will put the research library world on a new plane with regard to eventual control of commercially-produced microform sets.

As a small library in a bibliographic utility, the likelihood of acquiring microform sets would be increased if bibliographic information were more readily available on-line.

It is important that the level of cataloging is "full" in accordance with AACR2 if the project is to elicit a wide participation. It is also crucial to enter the data into a data base such as OCLC especially because many large academic libraries are planning for on-line catalogs in the next two to three years.

We rely on published guides, publishers' reel lists, brochures, etc. as much as possible. Analytic cataloging is supplied only if available for purchase -- past practice. Current practice -- recently purchased analytic cards are not being processed because of the need for authority work and/or tagging for data base entry and lack of space in public card catalog. All analytic cards which had been in the shelf list have been removed due to lack of cabinet space.

Our records are very poor. Some collections are not cataloged at all -- the staff just know they exist. Some collections only have analytics filed, but may not have analytics for all of a collection. It is difficult to track down what we have done. Just identifying the titles we own has been a major accomplishment. Because [library] will benefit greatly from the success of the project, we may be willing to reconsider cooperation on a title by title basis for new titles. Please keep us informed.

Quite frankly I have too many other things to think about getting controlled before we can think about some of our microform sets.

Shared cataloging from LC and OCLC member institution bibliographic records is an important factor in formulating our cataloging policies and priorities. And, as we rely upon access to records for our use, we consider our participation important also. Microform sets are not at the top of our list of cataloging priorities to be sure, but our participation in shared cataloging of this material is definitely an on-going activity. Therefore, the prospect of participation in a cooperative cataloging project is an interesting consideration. Please accept this as an indication of our willingness to consider a formal arrangement for cooperative cataloging of microform set(s), dependent upon the provisions of such an arrangement, of course, and the impact to our cataloging priorities and production.

Association of Research Libraries

MICROFORM PROJECT, 503 11th Street, S.E., Washington, D.C. 20003   (202) 544-0291

JEFFREY HEYNEN
Project Coordinator

April 30, 1982

Dear Librarian:

The enclosed survey initiates a major program of the Association of Research Libraries Microform Project. It is being sent to libraries in the United States and Canada to obtain detailed information regarding bibliographic control of microform sets. The survey's three-part questionnaire asks what sets are held, whether sets held have been cataloged and if so how, and what priority should be given for future cataloging. The forms also have questions on libraries' overall cataloging policies with regard to microforms and request that respondents indicate what sets they would be willing to catalog partially if other libraries were to catalog remaining portions and whether they would be willing to catalog certain sets were other libraries to catalog certain others.

Survey results will be used to help set priorities for cataloging, alert libraries to needless duplication of effort where it exists, help distribute cataloging work so that all libraries have opportunities to participate and no libraries are unfairly burdened, provide information on partial cataloging that has already been done, assist in putting together groups for shared cataloging programs, give data for use of publishers to promote cataloging of sets at source, provide information for grant applications by which libraries may obtain funds for cataloging projects, and coordinate efforts to establish cooperation between the bibliographic utilities for exchange of cataloging records.

Using the results, the Microform Project will set up an information clearinghouse to respond to specific questions on existing holdings and catalog records, and on plans for future work. It will also produce summary reports on sets that have been, are being, and will be cataloged and it will provide data for assessing the need for further programs to coordinate bibliographic control activities. All respondents will receive copies of the summary reports. They may also call or write the Microform Project office for responses to questions on specific information that the database contains.

Continued overleaf -

The three parts of the questionnaire are as follow:
(1) questions on microform cataloging policies, (2) questions on
holdings and the cataloging that has been given specific sets,
and (3) questions on priorities for future cataloging and
interest in participation in cooperative cataloging projects.
Only one copy of the first part should be needed. Please make
additional copies of the others if not enough of them have been
provided.

The survey greatly extends and brings up to date a pair of
surveys that were conducted for ARL by Information Systems Consultants Inc. in 1980. You may find that you have photocopies of
previous responses which may be used in completing the enclosed
forms.

Incidentally, a number of those who responded to the ISCI
survey reported that the forms served a useful internal record-
keeping function. You might consider their value as administrative tools for microform collection management. The lists of
titles and alternate titles of major sets may also be handy
reference tools.

I thank you very much for taking the time to read and
complete the survey. The parts may be returned to me as they are
completed. Please return the last of them by June 30th.

If you need more time or have any questions about the
survey, please contact me by letter or phone as promptly as you
can. The response forms have been deliberately kept as brief and
uncomplicated as possible. Sheets are provided for comments
where modification or elaboration of responses is needed.

A final note, if any of the information on your completed
survey should be considered confidential and used only without
attribution or with prior permission, please use the comments
sheet to specify which responses are private ones and what
guidelines should be followed in using them.

The Microform Project has been set up to assist libraries,
microform publishers, and the bibliographic utilities in achieving
bibliographic control over microform sets. If you would like to
receive more information on the project and to be placed on the
project mailing list, please put a mark in the box at the end of
the Part I of the questionnaire (Questions on Microform
Cataloging Policy).

Sincerely,

QUESTIONNAIRE, Part I

Questions on Microform Cataloging Policies

1. Does the library catalog some or all of the titles that are contained within large microform sets and/or provide full analytics for sets?

   Always _____   Sometimes _____   Never _____

2. If the answer to question 1 is Sometimes or Always, do you: catalog sets already held and/or catalog new acquistions?

   Catalog sets already held _____
   Catalog new acquisitions _____

3. Has the library in the past entered this cataloging into one or more machine-readable databases?

   Always _____   Sometimes _____   Never _____

4. Does the library continue to enter this cataloging into a machine-readable database?

   Yes _____   No _____

5. What database(s) have you entered or do you enter microform cataloging records into? (If possible, indicate years during which entering was done.)

	Formerly	Currently
OCLC	_____	OCLC _____
RLIN	_____	RLIN _____
WLN	_____	WLN _____
UTLAS	_____	UTLAS _____
Unique in-house System	_____	In-house _____
Other	_____	Other _____

6. If the library catalogs titles within microform sets as they are acquired, do you keep records showing what sets receive cataloging and how many titles have been cataloged?

   Yes _____   No _____

Continued overleaf -

7. Does the library use catalog cards supplied by publishers when they are available?

   Always _____   Sometimes _____   Never _____

8. If the library does use catalog cards supplied by publishers, are these records substantially revised before being used?

   Always _____   Sometimes _____   Never _____

9. Check here if you wish your name and address placed on the Microform Project mailing list   ____
                                                                      |____|

   Respondent Name _____

   Title/Department _____

   Library _____

   Institution _____

   NUC Symbol (if known) _____

Comments: _____

_____

_____

_____

_____

_____

Return completed form by **June 30th, 1982.**

Return to: Jeffrey Heynen, Coordinator
           ARL Microform Project
           503 Eleventh St. SE
           Washington, DC 20003   Tel (202) 544 0291

QUESTIONNAIRE, Part II

Questions on Holdings and Cataloging of Specific Microform Sets

In addition to this sheet, there are four items in this part of the questionnaire: a response form having a grid pattern on one side and a comments sheet overleaf together with three supporting elements.

The item on the back of this sheet is an explanation of the column headings that appear on the response form grid. It tells how the form should be filled out. Following it is the response form itself.

The remaining three items (labeled A, B, and C) give information on microform sets that is needed in completing the response form. Part II, A is a thirteen-page list of set titles. In addition to the titles themselves it has publisher notations and two key numbers: a four-digit code number and a serial number.

To save space and time and to avoid confusion, these two numbers are to be used in citing sets rather than the sets' titles. As the brief introduction to the title list states, the titles of microform sets are frequently difficult to pin down; assigning each of them a pair of unique numeric descriptors is a means of providing short, conclusive identifiers. (Using two identifiers rather than simply one provides a means of catching transpositions and other errors that might occur in filling out the form.)

Accompanying the list of titles are a brief list of publishers -- many of which have been cited only by initials or very compressed names in the title list -- and a seven-page list of cross references that provides alternate versions of microform set titles. The cross references are particularly useful for sets that do not appear to possess authoritative titles, but are variously cited by their publishers, reviewers, and users. These two items are Parts II, B and C, respectively.

The comments sheet on the back of the response form is to be used to expand upon answers given on the form and to provide information concerning major microform sets of monographs and completed serials in the library's collections whose titles are not given in the title list (and thus for which four-digit codes and serial numbers are not available).

Please photocopy the response form/comments sheet if additional copies are needed.

Response forms may be sent back as completed and need not be held until all sets in the library have been entered. Please return the **last** form no later than **June 30th** or contact Jeffrey Heynen at the address given on the form if more time is required.

Continued overleaf -

QUESTIONNAIRE, Part II -- Holdings and Cataloging Response Form

Explanation of Column Headings

Hold Entire Set - Put a check mark here if library has all parts published, publishing has ceased, and holdings are complete.

Hold Approx __% of Set - For sets incompletely held and not still being received, give approximate percentage held.

Still Receive Portions - Put a check mark if set is still being acquired on standing order or subscription (but not if you intend to acquire additional, but entirely separate parts for which different code numbers are given).

Have Prepared Local Finding Tools for Set - Put a check mark if library has prepared finding tools other than catalog records for titles in the set.

Have Cataloged Titles in Set - Put a check mark if the library has cataloged, or analyzed, all of the titles that the set contains.

Cataloging Continues - Put check mark if cataloging of this set is still in process.

Approx % of Titles Cataloged - Give approximate percentage of titles owned that have been cataloged.

Main Source of Cataloging Copy - Put a "P" if publisher's copy was the main source, an "N" if NUC/LC was the main source, a "B" if records from a bibliographic database (apart from publisher's or LC copy) were the main source, and an "X" if another source was the main one.

Cataloging Code - Identify code followed, using "P" for pre-AACR2 and "2" for AACR2. Put "X" if code is neither of these.

Level of Cataloging - State, broadly, whether records are full, minimum level, or brief. Definitions: "Full" means in accordance with your library's policies for full cataloging . "Minimum level" means using the national level minimum level standard for bibliographic records. "Brief" means cataloging that is neither full nor national level minimum level. Use "F" for full, "M" for minimum level, and "B" for brief. Put a note on the comments sheet if a more specific response is desireable.

% Entered Into Database - Give approximate percentage of titles owned for which records have been entered into an in-house machine-readable database or a multi-library database such as OCLC, RLIN, WLN, or UTLAS.

Entering Continues - Put a check mark if records continue to be entered into a multi-library database on an ongoing basis. If this is part of a retrospective conversion project, please note on comments sheet.

Hold Tape(s) Locally - Put a check mark if Library holds machine-readable records locally for items entered into a multi-library database.

Specify Database(s) - State database into which records have been entered. Use "O" for OCLC, "R" for RLIN, "W" for WLN, "U" for UTLAS, "I" for in-house. Put "X" for other. Put more than one letter if more than one database has been used.

QUESTIONNAIRE, Part II

Holdings and Cataloging Response Form

Four Digit Code	Item No.	Hold Entire Set	Hold Approx % of Set	Still Receive Portions	Have Prepared Local Finding Tools for Set	Have Cataloged Titles in Set	Cataloging Continues	Approx % of Titles Cataloged	Main Source of Cataloging Copy (P, N, B, X)	Cataloging Code (P, 2, X)	Level of Cataloging (F, M, B)	% Entered Into Database	Entering Continues	Hold Tape(s) Locally	Specify Database(s)

Photocopy this sheet if additional copies are needed.

Key: P = Publisher, N = NUC/LC, B = Bibliographic Utility, X = Other
     P = Pre-AACR2, 2 = AACR2, X = Other
     F = Full, M = Minimum Level, B = Brief (i.e. not F or M)
     O = OCLC, R = RLG/RLIN, W = WLN, U = UTLAS, I = In-House, X = Other

----

Please return forms **as completed** and return last form by **June 30th, 1982** at the
latest (contact Jeffrey Heynen at address given below if more time is needed).

Name of respondent _____
            Title _____
     Telephone No _____
          Library _____
      Institution _____
NUC Symbol (if known) _____

Return to:
Jeffrey Heynen, Coordinator
ARL Microform Project
503 Eleventh St, SE
Washington, DC 20003

(202) 544-0291

QUESTIONNAIRE, Part II

Comments

Four
Digit   Item
Code   No.   Comment

_____

_____

_____

_____

_____

_____

_____

_____

_____

_____

_____

_____

_____

_____

_____

_____

_____

_____

[Note: Sets for which four digit codes and item numbers are not available
should be cited by title and publisher. Please photocopy this sheet if
additional copies are needed.]

QUESTIONNAIRE, Part II, A - C

    Questionnaire Part II, A, B, and C are, respectively, a List of Titles, a
List of Publishers, and a List of Alternate Titles.

    Because these lists are given in fuller and more useful form in
Appendices D and E, they are not included here. The List of Titles that was
given with Part II of the Questionnaire contained the titles of 483 sets
derived from two sources: research done by Suzanne Dodson for the second
edition of her Microform Research Collections: A Guide and titles solicited
from Microform Publishers. The list given in Appendix D contains an
additional 361 sets contributed by responding libraries. The List of
Alternate Titles that was given with Part II is found in Appendix D merged
with the proper titles in a single alphabetical listing. The List of
Publishers is found at the end of Appendix D. Appendix E contains 35 sets
which were originally given in the List of Titles that accompanied Part II but
for which no libraries reported holdings.

QUESTIONNAIRE, Part III

Priority List

Please use this form to list the microform sets that your
library considers to be most in need of cataloging because of
their importance. Identify sets by their four-digit codes and
item numbers on the back of this sheet. Please give full titles
and publishers' names of sets you list that are not given on the
title listing.

The form asks for preferences ranked between 1 and 5.
One denotes lowest priority. Give a ranking of 5 to sets that
your library considers to deserve highest priority.

Insofar as you can, please also indicate whether your
library is willing and able to participate in cooperative
projects with other libraries to catalog these sets and use the
place provided for comments to state whether you would catalog
one or more sets provided one or more other libraries cataloged
other sets that you would like to see cataloged.

Please return completed form by **June 30th, 1982.**

Return to:

Jeffrey Heynen, Coordinator
ARL Microform Project
503 Eleventh St., SE
Washington, DC 20003

(202) 544-0291

QUESTIONNAIRE, Part III

Priority List

Four Digit Code	Item No.	Recommended Priority for Cataloging (1 to 5)	Interest in Coop Project? (Y or N)	Four Digit Code	Item No.	Recommended Priority for Cataloging (1 to 5)	Interest in Coop Project? (Y or N)

[Note: Sets for which four digit codes and item numbers are not available should be cited by title and publisher.]

The responses on this sheet reflect ...

Library policies, plans, or schedules for cataloging _____
Library informal goals _____
Departmental policies or informal goals _____
Personal view of the person responding _____

Comments _____

_____

_____

_____

_____

_____

_____

Name of Respondent _____

Title/Department _____

Library _____

Institution _____

NUC Symbol (if known) _____   Telephone _____

Key: 1 = Lowest priority; 5 = Highest priority